Surviving
SECONDARY
TRAUMA

From Struggle to Strength

by Janet Redford

Edited by Colleen Kern

Published by: GWN Publishing
www.GWNPublishing.com

Cover Design: Kristina Conatser

ISBN: 978-1-965971-00-0

FOREWORD

J anet has been writing this book, in one form or another for over a decade. Early on I watched her take two steps forward towards healing, and three steps back. As her thoughts and feelings evolved, and she entered a less debilitating stage of grief, she began to focus on not only her mental health, but the mental health of all folks that have suffered trauma or are close to someone that has. Thoughts of helping others pick up the pieces from experiencing trauma first-hand or as a secondary survivor, crept in and were formulated. The healing process had begun.

The effect trauma has on the victim really goes without saying, what sometimes gets lost in the shuffle is the toll it takes on the family, friends, and support personnel surrounding the victim. Janet has been able, although it has been a long arduous journey, to heal herself with the skills she has developed. At first, she coped, then she healed. Now, she is healing others.

This book can be difficult to read at times, due to the trauma our daughter experienced, but it is real life, real struggles, and real healing. I applaud my wife for taking the chance to open herself up to the reader and connect on multiple levels, all the while still healing. We are very lucky to have someone with immeasurable strength, not only take you through the process, but do it in such an honest and caring way.

The healing processes and skills Janet outlines within the book, work. They are time tested and have proven valuable to not only my families' secondary survivors, but in many ways have helped our daughter as we have healed so that we can effectively support her. This process is analogous to putting your oxygen mask on before you help others if your plane is going down. One can't truly help you survive unless they survive. That's the basic premise, heal yourself so you can heal others. Then she furthers the process from surviving to thriving. It can be done.

Janet and I are examples of successful healing to the stage of thriving in this life. I'm grateful for that and am thankful that what we went through didn't destroy our marriage or our relationships with our son and daughter. But mostly, I am proud. Proud that my wife courageously wrote this book for the benefit of others. Proud that from the ashes of what once was, a pillar of strength now stands. That pillar was erected for those in need, a way to cope, a way to mend, and a way to flourish.

Note from author: *I want to be completely honest with you. It's not typical for an author to ask their spouse to write the Foreword for their book. I asked my husband, Duane Redford, to write it because no one knows my voice better than he does. He has lived through this with me. When trauma impacts a family, it threatens the very existence of it and the relationships involved. We made a promise to each other, early in the trauma, that we would preserve our relationship with each other and our children. We weren't going to give trauma the ground between us. We didn't arrive at our marriage this way—we carved it out of the very terrain we walked individually and together. This is our Talisman—to never give up no matter what happens in life and to have each other's back. We are unstoppable.*

DEDICATION

*I dedicate this book to **YOU**, the reader.*

*For whatever reason, you chose to pick
up this book and read it.*

I believe people either know of, or are, a secondary survivor.

*I will never know the ripple effect,
and yet I know a ripple has begun in more than one life.*

*If I can help one person gain understanding that can support and shorten an individual's or family's length of pain,
then I have accomplished what I have set out to do.*

*I also dedicate this book to ALL Survivors,
Secondary Survivors and the generations that follow
knowing that trauma can travel generationally.*

I hold space for your healing.

"The expectation that we can be immersed in suffering and loss daily and not be touched by it is as unrealistic as expecting to be able to walk through water without getting wet."

—NAOMI RACHEL REMEN, MD

TABLE OF CONTENTS

Foreword 3

Introduction 9

Screaming in Silence 13

Secondary Survivor 21

50 Shades of Perpetrator 25

Looking Through the Mask 35

Name, Rank, and Serial Number 47

The Internal Perpetrator 53

Dying Moments 61

Getting Off the Ride 71

Customizing Support 79

The Ebb and Flow of Healing 97

The Internal Compass 107

Affirmations + Manifesto 119

Manifesto: Surrendering to Your Dreams —Your Sacred
Blueprint 125

Thank You! 127

Namaste 129

Acknowledgments 131

Author Bio 133

References 135

"Out of suffering have emerged the strongest souls; the most massive characters are seared with scars."

—KHALIL GIBRAN

INTRODUCTION

L ife often inflicts unexpected blows. For our family, the unexpected blow was delivered the day we found out our daughter had been a victim of sexual abuse. Learning of your child's trauma traumatizes you as well, by the sheer reality and impact of their experience. This secondary impact rings throughout the lives of the victim's loved ones whether it's sexual abuse or another type of trauma. As of this writing, I want you to know that my daughter is safe and continues to navigate her life. However, let me be clear: our journey, flawed by behaviors of self-sabotage and fear, has been far from easy. There were moments so dark they seemed to swallow us whole.

I need to warn you: parts of this book will be difficult to read. The intensity of some moments may feel overwhelming, just as they did for us. There were days when the weight of our pain felt crushing—when everything was at a ten. But here's what I've learned; you DO get through it. The intense moments pass. It's important to recognize when you're at a ten, but also when you're at a five, a two, or somewhere in between. It's about noticing the sun, choosing to look up rather than retreat into the familiar darkness of your mind because trauma plays the story over and over again. It's about loosening the grip that trauma has on your thoughts.

Healing doesn't follow a straight path; it flows like a mountain river, sometimes rushing over jagged rocks, other times slowing into calm pools. The key is learning to navigate the current, understanding that no rapid, no matter how fierce, lasts forever. Along the way, you'll find that life is not just intense and painful. Life also includes light, love, laughter and more that you never thought you'd experience again.

Healing also doesn't have to look a certain way. There's no set path you must follow; it only needs to be *your* way. Healing, elusive as it may seem, requires more than time; it demands committing to self-work, creating customized support, scheduling self-care, and above all, trusting yourself. It's not about confidence; it's about courage. The courage to take the next step that feels right for you. If something isn't helping, if it's making you feel worse, then stop. Get out. Even if all you can say is, "This makes me feel bad," listen to that. Trust your judgment. While my initial exposure to trauma therapy was negative, that doesn't mean all therapy is wrong. I've experienced profound healing through shifts guided by therapists, healing modalities and healing practitioners. The most important thing I've learned is that true healing happens when you trust yourself.

I write these words not only to recount my own struggles but to underscore a fundamental truth: words wield power. The notion taught in our youth that, "sticks and stones may break my bones, but words will never hurt me," is a fallacy. I've seen how harsh judgments make the pain worse, making it harder to navigate our healing. When you're focused on just surviving each day, clear thinking becomes a precious resource, one that's often stripped away.

This book is my attempt to illuminate the often overlooked condition and circumstances of secondary survivors—those friends and family members who stand alongside the wounded, grappling with their own trauma in the shadows. Our grief, isolation, and anger may be invisible to the world, but they are no less real. Let this be a testament to the immense weight that accompanies such a journey.

I am a mom whose little girl was sexually abused by the son of a family friend. What follows is my perspective and personal story, as unique as my fingerprint. My story may have similar patterns and appearances to others, but it will remain my own...what I identify with and what identifies me...it is also part of what made me who I am today. For me, writing is not just a means of expression; it is a lifeline, lighting the path toward healing. Through my words, I confront my own brokenness, piecing together fragments of my shattered self.

Kintsugi is a Japanese art in which broken pottery is repaired with precious metals, imbuing it with a new beauty—a beauty born of resilience and restoration. Likewise, I see my journey as a continuous process of mending, acknowledging the irretrievable losses while embracing the newfound strength in my scars. This is my path toward healing—a path that isn't easy—a path that is powerful.

My hope for you, dear reader, is that you too find solace within your broken spaces. That you gather the scattered pieces of your soul and embark on a journey of self-repair. For within you, lies the power to transcend the role of a secondary survivor—to reclaim your life, more beautiful and more resilient than before.

Step into your life, embody all of you at the soul level. You are more than a secondary survivor; you are a living testimony to the human spirit's extraordinary capacity for transformation.

"Trauma is personal. It does not disappear if it is not validated. When it is ignored or invalidated the silent screams continue internally heard only by the one held captive."

—DANIELLE BERNOCK

SCREAMING IN SILENCE

June 9, 2002

The last thing I remember before my world imploded was sitting in the church sanctuary waiting for service to begin. My husband gently taps my leg, signaling me to follow him. I looked over to see an usher quietly talking to him. I get up, exit the pew and follow them out of the sanctuary. Puzzled, I stay focused on the usher's back, wondering, what's going on? Why are we being called out of service—it's just about to start? We're taken down the stairs and into our associate minister's office where she is waiting for us.

I sit down, still confused why we are here. I look at her, her mouth begins to move and suddenly, I experience a DEAFENING explosion. I can't hear. My mind is filled with screaming as my mind, body, and soul shatter.

She has just told us that our 12-year-old daughter has been a victim of sexual abuse. I can't hear. I can't think. I can't see. The explosion was ME, my heart shattering. I'm screaming... my mind is screaming: No! No! No! No! No! Not my *baby*!

Please, GOD!

NOOOOOOOOO!!!!!!

Please, God……….…….no…. My body is buzzing, my ears are ringing, and I have lost my bearings. I can no longer see. I know our minister is in front of us, but I can't see her. I can only feel her presence. My husband is somewhere to my left, but I can't see him either. All I can feel are the sensations of my body telling me something HORRIFIC has just happened—something my brain refuses to logically register.

My soul writhes with the pain, trying desperately to hold onto the pieces of my heart that are screaming for help! Suddenly, I begin to feel more than the pain. The emotions are returning and beginning to build their own pressure. It feels like I'm going to lose it, break, fall apart, and disintegrate into oblivion because all that's left of me is in pieces. I am broken.

Then as if we are not shattered enough, we're blindsided by another blow. We are informed that our daughter's perpetrator is someone we know, the son of a family friend, a church member. It was a young man we had deeply trusted and supported for almost his entire life. I am beyond devastated; it numbs me. I can't take in any more information. I am beyond my capacity to feel, and I cease to exist in this moment.

After these horrifying revelations, our minister steps out to get our daughter and my tears begin to form. I can feel the internal scream starting to rise to the surface. My body is trembling. I try to catch my breath feeling my body starting to give way to the internal tidal wave threatening to take me under. My husband places his hand on my shoulder and whispers my name, stopping the tidal wave and forcing it to recede into the deepest crevices of my heart, locking it away in a vault. Everything is hushed, the air is silent and thick as my body continues to buzz.

The time has come to stand up so we can leave. I don't want to leave! I don't want to stand up! If I stand up, it means I'll have to go out that door and I don't want to go out that door. I'll walk out of any door but *that* door! Don't make me walk out that door! Please, God, don't make me walk out that door! My soul is sobbing, knowing, that if I go out *that* door it means I have to close the door to the life I had. I don't want to close that door! I want to keep that door open. Don't make me go out that door. Don't make me face this dark world! God help me! I don't want to leave!! I want you to give me back my life. GIVE ME BACK MY LIFE!! I'm silently screaming, my soul is screaming......... my mind is screaming...PLEASE GOD...NOOOOOO! I hear nothing.

I find myself at the door's opening and my daughter's face is in front of me. I hug her. I can see in her eyes that she has changed too, knowing that we know. She looks up at me. She is so quiet, so small, so vulnerable, so innocent. I can see the intense pain in her eyes, and it jars me. Her face burns into the deepest part of my soul. I will NEVER forget that look.

As we walked up the stairs, I stopped to look around. It feels like I've put on a mask and I'm peering through its eyes, seeing the same stairs and hallway as before, but I am no longer attached to my life in this moment. I can't feel. My heart has been obliterated from the explosion, and yet I am walking away... walking away from the life I knew. Walking away from the office where our former life, our GOOD life, exploded and tore through every inch of the room, leaving it splintered and unrecognizable. The same room where my soul remains, pulsing with pain and leaving me trying to breathe. I no longer exist. My life no longer exists.

I am moving in slow motion. Everything feels like it is in slow motion. I look around and everything is pristine, and in its place, adding to my confusion. We've just experienced an explosion. Why is everything in place? How can it be? What just happened? Why aren't the walls all shattered? Where's the debris? Where is everyone? What just happened?!

I don't remember much more from that day like how we got our son, got to the car, or even got home. I don't remember if we ate or where each of us went in the house. I don't remember sleeping or going to work the next day. I don't remember. I don't remember anything for… days, maybe weeks. I don't know. I just recall the constant buzzing in my brain, my thoughts racing, and being unable to stop the screaming inside my head. It was deafening and I couldn't take the mask off.

Okay…Breathe

Let's all take a breath, in and out, breathe. Simply writing this memory, even after twenty plus years, has my heart pounding and moved me to tears. So, I take a deep breath and I breathe. I invite you to join me and do the same. After writing out my memory, I talked with my family about their own memories of that day. They each recalled different parts of the day.

My daughter said she could still see us at the office, as if it were happening right now. She could see our faces; she could feel it. My son remembered being brought into the office, sitting on top of the desk, and watching me cry. Someone had told him something had happened to his sister. He didn't quite understand everything going on because he was 8-years-old. I had no recollection of my son being brought into the office or even of me crying. My husband only remembers the sensation of being blindsided, his body vibrating, and seeing only a vignette of our minister. He has no other memory.

None of us can remember going out to our car or how we got home. None of us remembers the rest of the day.

My son, now an adult, expressed a very important detail. He thought we had "the perfect life" until that day; afterward, it no longer existed. He said that our world got turned upside down and what made this so awful is that we only saw a sliver of the world his sister was thrown into years before we found out—and our small glimpse into her experience was horrific.

Meeting Your Basic Needs

Finding out your loved one has suffered sexual abuse is very traumatic. Your mind is racing, and thoughts come faster than you can process. There are parts of you that feel completely numb while other parts of you are in deep, constant pain. You want to feel safe yet feel very vulnerable. My husband and I quickly moved into protection mode. We didn't know what to do, so we did what we could. We isolated ourselves and tried to protect our daughter and son as much as we could.

From our experience, we learned many lessons in what to do and what not to do. My intention is to share our mistakes and successes so that you are able to shorten your length of suffering. We found that there is indeed a tipping point between protecting yourself and creating a self-imposed prison. The transition for us was so smooth that hindsight might be the only way we recognized it. Our goal is to help you avoid that tipping point.

What do you need? There are numerous answers and options. I've learned posing a few positive "what ifs" help me determine what I need from moment to moment so that I can work through the emotions and thoughts flooding my mind. Do you need to write out the ticker tape that's going on in your brain? What if you bought a journal so you could be free to write, draw, and express whatever you need to say without fear of judgment or getting it right? What if it's okay to make it as ugly as you need to make it, so you experience release? What if you install a punching bag in your garage or laundry room that allows you to release the physical stress that you're feeling? My husband added one in our basement to help reduce stress.

What if you made a list of different options that can help you EXPRESS or RELEASE thoughts, emotions, and stress? If you do, you'll have something to reference when stress takes over and it's hard to recall your healthy strategies. Here are some starters:

- Therapy: Talk therapy, equine gestalt therapy, somatic movement, EMDR, etc.

- Energy work: Cranial Sacral, Ortho-bionomy, Intuitive Medium sessions, etc.

- Breathwork: There are multiple breathwork exercises and apps to guide you.

- Meditate: There are many types of meditations available on apps.

- Private journal: Express whatever you need to express. For your eyes only.

- Go to an angry room: These are businesses that allow you to safely break things.

- Use a punching bag to physically release tension, stress, emotions.

- Throw ice cubes at the ground to shatter something safely.

- Scream into a pillow.

- Yell out a Tarzan call.

- Volunteer: It helps focus your thoughts elsewhere, allows you to help and connect with others.

- Work in a yard or garden to get your hands dirty and connect to Mother Earth.
- Go for a walk by yourself, with a friend, or walking group.
- Play a sport for a mental break and different focus.
- Exercise: Run, bike, swim, yoga, etc.
- Do something that feels productive to you.
- _____? (Build your own list.)

It's crucial to have a variety of options when you're not feeling your best and seeking ways to heal. Having choices allows you to ground yourself in the present moment, reminding you that this too shall pass. This one moment WILL pass. For me, meditative walks have been an invaluable tool to reduce stress and self-regulate. One of the most profound healing experiences I've had was through equine gestalt work—there's a depth to this work that transcends words, enabling powerful shifts and releases. Horses offer a unique sense of safety; their presence is free from judgment, providing only truth, validation, and healing. On days when I found myself being too serious, I would channel my inner Carol Burnett and let out a Tarzan call. If you're unfamiliar, a quick YouTube search will fill you in. This humorous release not only alleviated the tightness in my chest but it also brought laughter, helping me to lighten up when I was taking life too seriously. Having a range of options at your disposal is essential, as each one offers a different path toward healing and resilience.

*"Secondary trauma can trigger
buried memories of primary abuse
and trauma experiences."*

—DR. BILL TOLLEFSON

SECONDARY SURVIVOR

L et's start the conversation about "secondary survivors." While I was researching trauma, I came across these two words and felt an immediate resonance with them. The words alone provided an identity for my experience. People intuitively know about victims and perpetrators. What's often overlooked are the family or friends who live with the survivor in the aftermath and all its collateral damage.

Before I decided to use this term, I sat with my daughter to get her feedback on the phrase. She likened it to second-hand smoke, stating that it is nothing like what the victim experiences; it's separate yet interrelated. The experience smells, tastes, and feels different, yet is still intricately and irrevocably linked to the traumatic event. She said, it's like how second-hand smoke leaves its own impact on the people exposed to it. Her experience was her experience at the deepest core level, and she knew it had an impact on all of us just by being exposed to the essence of what she had experienced.

I thought this was a great analogy. Let's clarify it further to help define a secondary survivor. In our analogy second-hand smoke represents all of the particles of trauma that a victim emits from their abuse—behavior changes, sleep disturbances, emotional outbursts, depressive episodes, suicide ideations, and triggers from Complex PTSD. You can see it, smell it, and taste it. You have no control over it—it goes where it wants to go, and it impacts everyone who encounters it differently. The perpetrator has rolled their victim up in their toxic world and sucked the very life out of their victim, only to toss them away as trash when they're finished, with little care for the damage left in their wake.

My daughter's terror and trauma will never, ever be fully understood by us because only she has lived it in every cell of her body. How can she or any survivor come even close to sharing all they experienced. We may hear bits of their stories, if they're willing to share. We find the stories horrific, and they fuel our own nightmares. And yet, the victims frequently save us from every detail they have experienced... knowing it would also change us, knowing our understanding would still never match their own. However, this doesn't negate our own trauma in witnessing their lives crumble and change before our eyes.

Just Surviving

Trauma and tragedy have a ripple effect. How could I not be affected? How could I not feel the pain? How could I not be torn-up inside? How could it not shatter my life? My little girl loved the outdoors, loved animals, babies, children, chocolate, and she especially loved playing with her little brother. They were the dynamic duo who played and laughed together. I couldn't ask for better children. After that day, our little girl no longer existed. She felt exposed, as if a spotlight was following her, feeling very unsafe. So, she started to find ways to hide out.

As a mom, the pain I felt was overwhelming, the deepest I've ever experienced. It cut into me from two directions: the unbearable reality that my child had been traumatized and the helplessness of knowing I couldn't change what had happened... I felt completely lost, unsure of how to cope with this immense pain or how to help her. She was lost in her own world of suffering, and no matter how hard I tried, I couldn't reach her. She wouldn't let us in.

The particles of trauma started seeping out at a faster rate and I was starting to be overcome by it all. Life delivered the unexpected and somehow, we were still supposed to get up and do life every day. It was the last thing I wanted to do; I didn't want to get up or even wake up. I wanted to crawl into a cave, close my eyes, and never feel this pain again. I wanted this life to go away and never come back, to sleep until I woke up in our former life; a life I loved.

We were not yet survivors. We were just trying to survive.

"Perpetrators of abuse thrive in silence and secrecy. It is only when we speak out and hold them accountable that we can begin to break the cycle of violence."

—LUNDY BANCROFT

50 SHADES OF PERPETRATOR

Rarely are the identifying criteria of a perpetrator at one end of a spectrum or the other: it's not black and white, there's 50 shades of gray and beyond. Way, way, WAY beyond! I wish I could say that my daughter's perpetrator was a monster and easily detectable because of it. However, that was not the case. He was a monster of the worst kind, those that hide in plain sight and smile nicely. He didn't seem obviously "sketchy" or untrustworthy; he wasn't the TV version of the "evil guy" we're all trained to be wary of and avoid. This was a young man who attended church every Sunday with his family in a suit and tie, appearing very cheerful and polite. He was the first one to open the door for you, offer to carry your things and help you unload items from your car, and was active at school and at church. In fact, my husband and I were his sponsors at different times for various mission trips. In appearance, he was a very active youth member who, we felt, made the world a better place; polite, responsible, and did what his mom told him to do. And yet, he was our daughter's perpetrator.

Unfortunately, unlike TV would like us to believe, the perpetrators of sexual abuse on a child are often more similar to us than different. That's what makes them terrifying, and how they are able to perpetrate offenses so easily. Perpetrators can be the most unsuspecting people and often are. They come from all walks of life as far as income levels, education, job experiences, and family history. They look like one of us—"us" being as unique as each individual and community.

We think of perpetrators as "Stranger Danger" or having a certain sinister profile of what perpetrators look like and act like when in reality they may look and act just like us, at least in appearances. Perpetrators play in the dark. That's the key. They groom us into thinking they are just like us, have similar beliefs, and the same worries and concerns as us. They are wolves in sheepskin clothing, hiding among us so that our internal alarms don't go off. They position themselves as belonging to our group so they can get closer to their victims and gain access. "The majority of perpetrators are someone the child or family knows."[1]

Child sex offenders are rarely strangers. They have made their way into the family's trusted circle by befriending the parents and their children. My husband and I trusted our daughter's perpetrator. He exhibited the highest quality act of "sheep-like behavior" one could ever find. He had our trust, he had a relationship with us and our children, which gave him access to our daughter at church, our home, friends' homes, as well as in his own home. He made us believe that he was trustworthy. Again, an offender's whole purpose is to gain access to the targeted child. They prey upon our trust and our vulnerability. They play in the dark to hide and conceal their actions; they are about GROOMING.

---

1   RAINN n.d.

Grooming

Our experience taught us about the minds of the perpetrators and just how powerful they are at playing in the dark. They are VERY strategic and influential in their actions. Our trust was manipulated for our perpetrator's gain. He wove a web of deception around our lives so that the perpetrator could trap our daughter. When we begin to understand the grooming that has been done to our child, and to us, we begin to release our own guilt and shame because this web was not of our making. This was so important for us to realize to help move toward healing.

The National Center for Victims of Crime states, "Grooming helps the offender gain access to the victim and sets up a relationship grounded in secrecy so that the crime is less likely to be discovered." Three of the main tenets of grooming are:

1. Identifying potential victims,

2. Gaining their trust, and

3. Breaking down their defenses.

Grooming steps include:[2]

- Identifying and targeting the victim.
- Gaining trust and access.
- Playing a role in the child's life.
- Isolating the child.
- Creating secrecy around the relationship.
- Initiating sexual contact.
- Controlling the relationship.

---

2   National Center for Victims of Crime n.d.

Our daughter's perpetrator was not just a friend, he was also her babysitter. His mother and I attended choir practice together, so she offered to have her son watch our children. I would drop my children off at his family's home every week believing they were safe and having fun. That was the role he played in my daughter's life—a position of trust, a caretaker of her and my son. We trusted him.

When he started abusing her, he isolated and controlled her with physical, aggressive harm and traumatic threats. She told us about one time when he grabbed her fingers with both of his hands, pulling her thumb and index fingers apart, as if to tear her hand in half. It was his way of forcing her to the ground. She felt pain and terror. MOTHER FUCKER! This is only ONE incident!!! He was very good at hiding what he was doing because neither his brother nor my son knew about the abuse. He was able to secure a safe place to commit his offenses. Even when his father was home, the abuse was still happening to my daughter. That's how skillful perpetrators are. They can offend even when people are around.

When our daughter's abuse was reported, my husband and I learned that only 2 percent of children tell. TWO PERCENT. The other incomprehensible fact is that, 1-in-4-girls and 1-in-6 boys will be sexually abused before they turn 18 years old[3]. This highlights just how skilled offenders can be at grooming, abusing and keeping their victims silent. They traumatize them into secrecy. They make the victim feel unsafe and threatened so that when they leave the situation, their dark secret is secured. The perpetrator must dominate their victim's mind, so they think and feel escape is impossible. What I learned from my daughter's trauma is

---

3   American SPCC n.d.

that she did everything she needed to do to survive her abuse and to keep herself alive.

We will never know exactly how perpetrators silence their victims because it is they who exploit the victim's fear. Some examples of the fears commonly exploited are:

- The perpetrator has threatened to harm or kill the victim if they tell.
- The perpetrator has brainwashed them to believe that it is their fault and so they are ashamed and embarrassed.
- The victim fears it's too dangerous to tell.
- The victim can't find a safe way to tell someone.
- The victim doesn't have a safe person to tell.
- The victim is scared that they won't be believed or will be blamed.
- They believe they are protecting the parents or a family member from being hurt.

Our daughter's perpetrator told her he would kill her if she told. He was securing secrecy and keeping our daughter captive. She was too scared to tell for fear of dying. He had control over our daughter's mindset and worldview. No matter what, she wasn't going to tell. It wasn't until two key elements came into perfect alignment that she was able to tell. Her perpetrator's presence in her life stopped and later she found a safe person to tell who did something about it. She wouldn't have been able to inform anyone if those two situations had not come together.

What led to her perpetrator no longer being present in her life? The family had stepped back from church and social events to deal with something privately. We didn't know what was going on, we just knew that they were pulling back. So, for months, my daughter no longer saw him at church, and I wasn't dropping my children off to be babysat. Her abuse came to an unexpected end...THANK GOD!

This was the turning point. She had time and space away from her abuser to figure things out, like who to tell. My daughter had told a school friend what was happening to her, but the friend didn't do anything about it. I believe children don't know what to do with this information. The friend didn't know that she should tell her mom or her dad. She was in elementary school and may not have even really understood what was going on. So, my daughter had to find someone else to tell.

Some of you might be wondering why our daughter didn't tell us. Parents often believe their child will tell them if someone is hurting them. They know they have a good relationship. That might be true. However, you don't know the case the perpetrator is building up against your child; what they're saying to them. A perpetrator's main goal is to keep their secret life undetectable. When a perpetrator tells the victim that they'll be killed, it's their fault that this is happening, that they are in some way at fault—a child doesn't want to tell their parents. They feel ashamed, embarrassed, vulnerable, and who knows what else. Our daughter later told us that she wouldn't have been able to bear seeing the hurt on our faces; to be responsible for our pain. She felt worthless, ashamed, and more importantly feared for her life.

One key tool I gave my children when they were young was repeated discussions on how to find a safe person to tell if someone was ever hurting them. As I drove them to activities, I would tell my daughter and son that if anyone was ever hurting them that they could come to me or their dad. I also shared with them that **IF** for whatever reason they felt they couldn't tell us then the next best option was to find a safe adult to help them. We discussed different people they could go to, who they thought were safe people, and identified them. The whole point of our conversation was to give my children options for getting help if they needed it.

I know as parents we want to believe that we will always be that safe person for our children. The thing is we don't think the way that perpetrators think. They have 50 shades of control, dominance, secrecy and beyond. The reality is that we need to connect as many lifelines to our children as we can. We need to help them build their own safety net of connections.

The Truth Revealed...

Once our daughter's abuse was reported to the police, we were instructed to go to the police station to meet with a detective assigned to investigate the case. Our daughter needed to come with us so they could interview her. We were not allowed to go with her. While she was being taken into the interview, my mind spun off in a million directions. Will she even be safe? What are they going to do to her? What kind of questions are they going to ask her? You feel so helpless.

In the meantime, the detective took down information from us to get details from what we knew. How did we find out about the abuse? Who reported it? More and more questions. Never were we told, "I'm sorry for what you're going through. Let me guide you as best as I can through this process, okay? Take your time." It was almost as if compassion was not allowed. You're just supposed to hear the question and answer it. It was mind-numbing. And then another blow was delivered to us, turning me into a stone statue blocking any more access to me. Our case was being added to an existing case that involved the molestation of two very young children: a 3-year-old and a 6-year-old.

We went through the process of meeting with the District Attorney and Victim's Advocate (VA). The attorney explained his approach and what he would do. The VA would keep us posted. We didn't get to participate much in what they were deciding; especially since we were getting added to the already existing case. Another victim was added on after us. We were expected to just blindly follow along.

The one thing I recall being able to contribute was writing a victim's impact statement. I couldn't sleep that night, so that was the night I wrote my impact statement. My husband wrote one as well. My daughter wasn't ready. She was still focused on surviving.

The court date arrived, and it was the first time, since they stopped coming to church, that we would see the perpetrator and his family. I was beside myself with anguish, it was nerve racking.

We sat in the courtroom, my heart pounding, my palms sweating, taking in everything in the room. Our daughter is to my right, and I have my victim's impact statement on my lap. The case is presented. The perpetrator gets up and makes his tearful apology that felt more about him being caught than feeling remorseful. Then it was our time to give our impact statement.

Every time I look back at this moment, I am angry. The entire time we gave our statements, the perpetrator's attorney was in a continuous conversation with him, so he didn't really have to listen to us. He was leaning toward his attorney to listen to him. Our daughter's perpetrator got 2 days in jail, a year probation, and was required to attend a sex offender program. Wow. Two days in jail and then freedom. My daughter has suffered a lot longer than that because of what HE CHOSE to do to her!

The system was very broken when we were going through this in 2002-2003, and I'm not sure how much it has truly improved. I believe the system is built more for the perpetrators than for the survivors and their families. They get endless support while victims receive a specified number of treatments. Survivors can continue to benefit from victim's compensation if they keep going to treatment. Immediate family members, at that time, got 12 sessions with a therapist or could attend a 12-week support group program. However, if any of you stopped going, then the compensation stopped.

My daughter went for a while and then stopped because it was too much for her. She was still trying to survive after telling; she didn't feel safe. Her anxiety and paranoia were increasing and her need to feel safe was her top priority at the time, understandably. She wasn't ready to process what happened to her. I don't blame her. I was still struggling with what *might* have happened to her, so I can't imagine her being ready to "go there" yet.

"We all wear masks, and the time comes when we cannot remove them without removing some of our own skin."

—ANDRÉ BERTHIAUME

LOOKING THROUGH
THE MASK

Betrayal delivers devastating blows. Betrayal isn't even a strong enough word to describe what the perpetrator did to my daughter's life. From the very first day that he sexually molested her, and all the time after, he turned her world upside down, feeding a storm inside of her. We could see her changing before our eyes. She wasn't the same person anymore.... And later? She would become lost in the storm.

The severe deception of our daughter's perpetrator crushed my worldview, my beliefs about God, and what I thought I knew about people. I was shattered and didn't know what to believe or who to trust. The betrayal took me off my feet. I didn't know what to do. I couldn't sleep; didn't sleep. I missed my old life. I didn't know this life and didn't want to know it. It was dark and silent. I felt so alone, and I couldn't talk about it. I got very good at compartmentalizing things—wearing my mask to keep me safe.

My husband and I were trying to protect our daughter and find safe ground for our son. We didn't want him to feel the storm the three of us were battling. We wanted him to be safe and untouched, but no matter how hard we tried, the storm swallowed him up too. More grief. Thicker mask.

I was stricken with grief. The sad part is that when traumatic situations happen and innocence is lost, there isn't a funeral. There's nothing in place that calls your community of friends and family together to surround you with love, support, and casserole dishes to help you cope with your grief and to help carry you through your pain. My daughter and son lost their childhood. My daughter lost her innocence, sense of safety, and more. We lost the best part of our lives and there was no ceremony to acknowledge our grief and help comfort us.

I can look back now, with hindsight, and realize our biggest mistake was choosing to stay silent and try to get through this on our own. It's hard to realize that in the moment because you don't know who to trust. The betrayal was too strong. We had chosen silence and isolation. We put our masks on, and because of that, we were alone. No meals. No one to sit with. We were left deep in our misery and our pain. We didn't have a place to go and bury our beloved family life that was so young when it died. We didn't have a place to pay our respects with flowers and to say how much we missed and loved that precious life.

Isolation

I was lost in so many ways. I didn't know how to feel. I couldn't feel sadness. I couldn't feel anger. I felt lost, distressed, and fearful, untethered from everything I knew, loved, and trusted. I was so scared for my daughter. Our family was caught in the chaotic whirlwind of the storm, tossed up with all its debris cutting into us, bruising us, and bringing even more pain to our already injured lives. We were trying to scream for help, but our isolation was the very storm that was carrying our voices away so no one could hear our screams. No one.

I was so scared to even begin to learn the details of my daughter's abuse. In all honesty, I don't believe I could've handled knowing, at that time. I was already having nightmares without details. Our daughter was living in silence, and she was far from telling us anything of her abuse. She needed to get as far away from it as possible just to feel safe… and year after year, she didn't feel safe. If anything, her sense of danger increased more and more as time passed.

My reaction was to commit to keeping my mask on so no one had access to my emotions or to me. I had to appear to be okay, to "be strong."

Shame

As a mother, I was ashamed that something like this happened to my little girl. I felt deep, deep guilt. Each week, I had driven her to be taken care of by someone who was abusing her. She must have felt that I was betraying her, as well, because I was the one taking her. She must have hated me or hated me now. I kept waiting for the day that my daughter would rage at me for taking her there. It was my fault. *I* had taken her. *I* had dropped her off. *I* had picked her up and didn't know that she was keeping a deep dark painful secret. My daughter, whose worldview was changed in an instant by terror, trauma, and shame rode home each week without me knowing of her struggle. God, how *I* hated me. How could I let something like this happen? How could I have not known?

Before we knew about her trauma, I was struggling with my daughter's choices and behaviors. It had started near the end of elementary school and continued into her first year of middle school. We would argue about the friends she was hanging out with, her mouthing off at home and starting to do poorly in school. All signs that something had changed.

In the evenings, I would talk with my daughter and ask her if someone was hurting her. She would shake her head no. I would ask again and reassure her it was okay to tell me. Still, she would say no. I felt like she was closing me out and I couldn't find a way to get in. It felt like she was standing inside her bedroom door, and I was on the outside trying to get her to open the door. And she wouldn't. She wouldn't open the door and let me in.

She had a lot of trouble sleeping at night. Sometimes her legs would tremble, so I would rub her legs until she fell asleep. Afterward, my husband and I would talk at length about her struggle to sleep, her behavior, and how we felt something was wrong. We both sensed it and were more than concerned. We'd sit up in bed racking our brains going over every place she was engaged in, or who she was around. We tried and tried to determine what might be causing her behavior, where she might be in danger.

My husband also tried talking with her, sat with her, and spent time with her. He'd ask if anyone was hurting her and tell her how she could tell us. We'd ask that repeatedly.

Perplexed as we were, we knew something was going on. Our daughter's behavior had changed. There was a point when we even approached her school to figure out what was going on. My husband called the school to investigate the cause and to see if any of her teachers knew something. I went to her school and talked with the school counselor to see what I could do to improve our relationship and help my daughter. We were looking at everything. We just weren't getting any answers as to why we were going through this with her. That is, until June 9th.

We got our answer.

Who Do I Tell?

One of your first thoughts when this happens is, who can I tell? My husband and I were so shattered by this. We wanted to protect our daughter, keep her safe, and felt paralyzed by not knowing our next steps. It felt safer keeping it to ourselves because at least we could control that. Everything else felt out of our control. If a family friend could inflict such deep pain, then who were we to trust?

Keep ourselves safe. That was our thinking. We chose not to tell any of our neighbors and told only a few friends without going into much detail. I know they heard us but I'm not sure they knew what to do with this painful information. Who does? No one is taught how to handle this type of situation. We're all left in the dark when sexual abuse occurs. We struggle to know how to be supportive and how to ask for support. The end result is radio silence.

When I chose silence and isolation, my emotions got placed in a vault and put on lockdown. There was no one to talk to and the outcome was living numb. I was surviving, but only at the most basic level. Our house became our fortress, sleep was nonexistent, and my husband and I were on autopilot, like robots; at least that was my experience.

The error we made was we created a self-imposed hell. We thought we were securing our safety when in reality by locking ourselves up in seclusion we only felt the pain more intensely *because* we were alone. We were living a life sentence that felt never ending. I know now, our biggest mistake was keeping our silence and staying in isolation which only supports the perpetrators of this world; not your survivor, yourself, or your family.

At the same time, our daughter's world was unraveling, and we were experiencing bigger pieces of her trauma. Once her abuse was revealed, she became very paranoid and anxious. She kept looking over her shoulder and felt in constant, present danger. Her bunk bed became a type of barricade, all sides completely blocked and protected. She wasn't sleeping and was endlessly exhausted, only letting herself sleep if one of us was sitting next to her on the couch, sitting on the floor next to her bed, or if I was laying with her in her bed. Sometimes she would sleep better during the day when the entire room was lit by sunlight, and we were all home. Other times she needed to be alone in her room with her door closed and one of us sitting outside her door all night. Sleepless nights went on for years. Even in her teens when she wanted to move her room to the basement, she still requested that her dad sit on the couch outside of her bedroom until she fell asleep. She needed to feel safe and actively protected.

What Do I Do About the Feelings I Had For "THEM?"

My husband and I also had to deal with the feelings about the perpetrator—what we thought we knew and what the reality was. We each handled it differently. I couldn't conjure up any emotions of anger. That was an emotional area of my life I had sealed away, way before this time in my life; so, my only response was to stay numb.

My husband, on the other hand, was not only devastated; he was enraged. Someone had hurt his little girl, and he wanted revenge. He wanted the perpetrator to feel the pain inflicted on our daughter, for him to hurt more than she was hurting. He wanted to get his hands on him! And one night he couldn't take it anymore and wanted to go get him. He was jumping up and down in pain and anger. He wanted to leave our house, drive to their house, and find him. It was a harrowing event to see my husband in this state. He was beside himself with grief, pain, and anger. I remember physically blocking the door and yelling out, "Who can I call?! Who can I call to come talk to you? Who can I call? What will help you?" He was so determined. He just kept jumping up and down. I started screaming, "You're no good to us in prison! You can't do this!!! We need you! You can't do this! Who can I call? Don't leave us alone in this! You're no good to us in prison... please... don't do this!" And after a while, the raging storm finally passed.

This is what's real. This is what happens in a house where the family is suffering with trauma and tragedy. We have every right to feel angry, to want to hurt or even want to kill the perpetrator, because they betrayed us at our deepest soul level, inflicting the most horrifying pain. It's alright for my husband to feel this way. What makes it excruciatingly difficult is not being able to do anything about what has happened to our child. We can't turn back the hands of time and stop it from happening. We can't change the truth—and that makes it unbearable.

What are we to do with this truth and the emotions or the lack of emotions that are attached to all of this? What do you do when the wall you've been building inside starts to come tumbling down? What happens when the internal build up reaches its tipping point? You explode. And that's what my husband needed to do. He had remained calm and silent for so long and was tending to the care of our daughter all the while trying to figure out how to deal with his emotions toward his daughter's betrayer. He needed to express the deepest part of his rage rather than let it eat him alive.

I felt guilty for not being able to feel anger...I couldn't bring it up. What was wrong with me? What kind of mother am I that I can't feel rage and anger toward the perpetrator? This completely shut me down.

This young man had been part of our life from the time his mother was pregnant with him. I had held him as a baby. I had seen him grow from a young boy into a young man. We engaged in his life at church and just a couple of years before my daughter's abuse we had started engaging socially outside of church with his family. A group of us had created a Potluck Club in which four of the five families had known each other since we were little, little children. Our perpetrator's family was the only family we had not grown up with... instead their children had grown up in front of us at church.

I struggled to work through my feelings because of this relationship with the family and their two sons. What was I to do with these relationships now? I couldn't deal with it. I felt so betrayed. And I felt like I couldn't trust any of them, especially the mom. Before we had found out about our daughter, she had shared with the women in our potluck group that her niece had accused her son of "touching" her. She had asked if I could imagine him doing that. I had replied that I couldn't and that I wouldn't even know how to respond to that. Then she went on to describe how her niece, a small young girl, displayed very sexual behaviors that were very questionable. Looking back now, it feels like I was groomed right out of any suspicion of her son. It was just months later that I would learn of my own daughter's abuse at the hand of her son.

After the way she had talked of her niece, describing her as the one to blame, I could no longer trust her. I imagine she was doing the same with all of her son's victims. Blaming them rather than her son; it was their fault. I couldn't go meet with them. I felt I would not get any truth out of the mom or anyone in the family for that matter. I let go of my feelings for this family—keeping myself numb. For now...I stayed numb...it was safer.

No Crying Allowed

Staying numb. That is what I was doing, staying numb. I had been brought up to not show my emotions and that showing emotion would put me in danger. I was to look or appear content and not let on or give any indication that I was confused, hurt or unhappy.

Staying numb served my mask well, but truly became the enemy to my healing. I had taught myself how to shove all my emotions into a box and hide it down so deep within me that it was more like an underground vault. No one knew it was there and I gave no indication of its existence.

I knew how to disconnect from my heart. This was a part of my own story growing up. Not showing emotions kept me safe and my daughter's trauma triggered a stricter practice of this safety response.

Survival mode was our standard. As parents we tried to figure out how to keep my daughter alive when she became suicidal. We dealt with this on an ongoing basis while she was in and out of therapy and other services. Even though, as a parent, I felt relief that she was getting the support and services she needed, there was another part of me wondering if my daughter was even ready for it.

I witnessed my daughter feeling extremely vulnerable and unsafe after telling of her abuse. Even though we, as a society, want them to talk it out, or work it out, and then be okay. It doesn't work that way. Healing takes time, a lot of time, and rushing them will never work. Some are not ready for therapy after they've just revealed the abuse. My daughter needed safety and distance first, period. Her therapists knew she could only go so far at the time and only so much progress could safely be made.

We also were given access to a therapist for our son, to make sure nothing had happened to him. Everything checked out fine as far as no sexual abuse to him, but we will never know how much collateral damage he silently incurred due to the storm in our family life. I know he carries scars, anger, misunderstandings, and more from this trauma. He will never get that part of his life back. He was completely innocent in his love for life, his joy, his smile, and the love he shared with us; only to have it shut down. I am deeply saddened by this because I feel my son grew up angry and resenting life. His life turned 180 degrees. We watched a young boy change from happiness and love to anger, frustration, and more that we probably cannot even comprehend. His worldview also got destroyed.

"When secondary survivors are treated as statistics rather than individuals, their pain is diminished, their voices silenced, and their humanity denied."

—UNKNOWN

NAME, RANK, AND
SERIAL NUMBER

My husband and I attended our own support group at an "advocacy" center that was located fairly close to the perpetrator's neighborhood. My heart would pound when we drove to the center because I was so afraid to see him or the family—even in another car. The group was specifically for parents of children who had been sexually abused. I was nervous about attending the group. I didn't know what it was going to look like or what we would be doing. I wanted to be able to talk with the other parents to share what we were going through, to know that we were not alone, and that our family was not alone. I wanted to feel safe again.

Upon our arrival, one of the therapists asked us to take a moment to fill out a questionnaire to test our knowledge on the signs of sexual abuse. My husband answered it with 100 percent accuracy; I passed in the 90th percentile. We both have experience working in the education system. The female therapist was almost shocked that we already knew so much of the information. Unfortunately, just being informed of the signs doesn't prevent abuse. The difference is that we think differently than the perpetrators. The questions should have asked us about grooming—the signs, behaviors, and approaches to be aware of. Even then, I feel like we would have failed that type of test. Innocent people do not think like perpetrators.

The support group was a 12-week program. It was covered by victim's compensation, so we decided to use my husband's compensation visits for this group. If you stopped going, you lost that compensation. So, once we committed, we needed to stick with it. I was so nervous and yet at the same time, I so badly wanted relief from our pain. I could feel hope when we started walking toward the building.

I wondered how they would get us started. Would the other families be people I could talk to? We sat around a large table with the other families with a male and female therapist leading the group. The therapists directed us to go around the table and introduce ourselves, state our name, the age of our child at the time of their victimization, and what had happened to them. That's it.

When I heard this, my throat clenched. I'd have to SAY what happened to our daughter. I'm going to have to say it out loud in front of a group of strangers. What?! Aren't we going to take time to get to know each other? Where's the icebreaker to help us ease into this group? Where's the safety? What?! Sure, these people might be experiencing what I'm experiencing, but I don't know them! And they don't know me! My mind swirled around the command: Name, rank, serial number. What am I, a fucking statistic to you? I'm having a hard enough time as it is, and NOW you're telling me say it OUT LOUD?!

When the time came for me to introduce myself, I couldn't. My body was buzzing, my mind was screaming, and I was shutting down. My husband introduced the both of us, and I don't even know what that did to him and his heart.

We repeated this drill every fucking week...no emotion please, just name, rank and serial number. That wasn't the worst part; the worst part always came after that. The therapists had us sit and watch videos, EVERY WEEK, of perpetrators and how they worked, how many children they had victimized and their mode of operation for abusing children. I remember one perpetrator stating he had sexually abused hundreds of children. Another talked about how he could molest a young girl right in front of her parents without them even knowing. From that moment on, I have no memory of any of the other videos. I just remember the screaming inside my head starting again; another explosion, another shattering. I was not safe. This dark world had tricked and betrayed me again. They had convinced me that I was going to get help getting out of this dark world. Instead, they grabbed my head and submerged me into the depths of hell and all the toxic devils that live there started to consume me.

We never got to talk to the other parents. I never got to talk. I never got to ask a question to the group. I just got to know their credentials of name, rank, and serial number. I was sitting in a group with other parents hoping to connect, to hear their story, to hear how their child or children were doing. I wanted to ask if their children were sleeping at night. Did any of their children have physical tremors? Did their children build a fort around their bed and barricade themselves at night? Did they look around and search for their perpetrator? Were they paranoid? Did they rage? Did their children take their rage out on them, the parents? I had so many questions. I wanted to talk about my pain and see if I was like them. Was I like someone in this situation? I felt all alone. Did they feel guilty that their child was victimized? I didn't get to ask. It was name, rank, and serial number then video time—showcasing all that is horrible in this world against children.

As I sat in a room with adults I didn't know and didn't connect with, by therapists' design, I felt so much pain and anguish. I was living in a nightmare; one that I couldn't wake up from. I don't even remember what the therapists looked like, their names, or for that matter anyone else in the room. Physically, I was there but more and more I began to leave my body whenever we went into that room; it felt never ending. It is no surprise that my husband had a gallbladder attack canceling our attendance at the final group meeting. Honestly, I was relieved. One less night of trauma to my heart and soul. One less night of explosions. One less everything….

What I had hoped to be a path toward healing turned out to dump salt into the deepest crevices of my pain. It almost debilitated me and my husband. My soul was so deeply injured during those eleven weeks that it almost pushed me all the way over the edge. I thought I was lost before; now I barely existed and was overwhelmed with hopelessness.

Name, Rank, and Serial Number

"The greatest battles we face are often the ones waged within ourselves, where our inner critic becomes the most formidable adversary."

—UNKNOWN

THE INTERNAL
PERPETRATOR

The mental storm of my daughter's trauma was getting stronger, and I was lost within it. What I was witnessing was unbearable. I was losing my daughter, and I was afraid I was never going to get her back. I feared one day she would blame me for everything and hate me for the rest of her life. I was so grief stricken. I couldn't stop the negative tapes that were playing in my head: "You're a failure as a mom. Horrible!" "You're worthless!" "Disgusting!" "You're a BAD mom!" The tapes were getting so loud that it was hard to hear anything else.

It's my belief that any time life delivers an unexpected blow, all that is unhealed within us becomes magnified. The judgments we have about ourselves; our core beliefs; the beliefs we were brought up with; they all become significant players during a mental storm. The judgments I had about myself were endless and I couldn't get away from them. You see, I was also sexually molested when I was a young girl. The day it happened, I went home and told my mom. She punished me. Yep, my mom punished me. I was deeply confused, so confused, so ashamed, and I felt so very, very alone. I don't even know if she ever told my dad. I was silenced.

As a child, I was not to show emotions. I was to "fix my face" and that's when I learned to put the mask on. Being young, the mask helped me to appear happy, good to go, and that nothing is wrong. It was not only a command growing up, but it was also, once again, my survival tool. What we don't understand is that over time, the mask weaves together multiple lies that keep us trapped in a web of pain. We become our own abuser. Our inner critic becomes an internal perpetrator that keeps us from reaching out for help, telling us untruths, and trying to dismantle the very person we came here to be. We're constantly battling ourselves; we think that we're crazy; that this is our life and that it's never going to end.

There is a tipping point when a person moves from survival mode into a self-imposed prison. We just don't know we're in prison because the transition is so gradual. Our environment and behavior slowly change over time, and we don't notice that we've become trapped. We don't realize we're getting comfortable in the chaos and that illusion of safety becomes our pay off. I feel many people are like me and tend to isolate themselves when they're in deep pain. Instead of reaching out, we try to go it alone. We don't want to burden anyone. We're afraid we'll be judged and blamed, that it's our fault. We start worrying about what other people think.

Think of a young girl who is running along joyfully when all of a sudden, she takes a hard fall to the ground. Her mind and body have been jolted and her knees, hands, and arms are scraped and bloody. You can see the initial shock in her eyes. She's wondering what just happened. And then the physical awareness of the pain moves in, and she begins to cry. Survival mode kicks in and she grips what is hurting most, and rocks back and forth, to release the pain through tears. A loved one moves forward, kneels to connect with her, helps soothe her pain, and to reassure that she will be okay. You see that after a while, she begins to calm down, get her bearings, and does what is necessary to get back up on her feet. This scenario represents a healthy survival response.

Many of us, as adults, don't practice those same steps. We're expected to skip over soothing the hurt, to deal with it, get right back up, and get over it. Let me introduce the internal perpetrator. In our scenario this would be like having a significant adult or authority figure come out screaming at the injured child, yanking them up, and telling them how stupid they were for falling. You can see it in the child's eyes, the confusion, and the pain, they aren't allowed to get their bearings and are shamed for their crying, wondering now if it's all their fault. The child's soul has laid back down on the ground rather than getting back on their feet, while the physical body disconnects to generate safety with the adult.

When our internal perpetrator kicks in we start getting in our own way because of the mental story we're telling ourselves. Our internal stories rule us, and we might not know that we can change them. We're still too steeped in the pain or are still laying on the ground from our fall.

This can create a breeding ground of self-destruction. I'm not going to lie; life was very hard during this time...more than can be described. Most people don't understand what secondary survivors' day-to-day life looks like or what's happening in all areas of someone's life. I was exhausted, my husband was exhausted, we were all exhausted. My husband and I still had to get up and go to work every day. Not something you want to do but have to do to keep your household going.

The financial burden is also beyond words. Family services are limited. The family members only get twelve sessions per person during this timeframe. That's not a lot, so then you're paying for your own therapy, you're paying for additional therapy when your child is ready to get help. Money is flying out the door, and you're doing everything you can to keep your child alive. I remember running into one of the moms from our "hell-support" group at my daughter's school. I never even knew we lived that close to each other.

I asked her how she was doing. She said that their child was taken off their husband's insurance because they had found out about the trauma and his mental health. Legal? No, but insurance companies are like fortresses or the Goliaths in the world who stomp on the small people. This couple also had to move from their dream home because their perpetrator lived next door. Our chat was short and was the only time we ever saw each other again. These are the things people don't realize are going on. You're not just dealing with the survivor's trauma; you're dealing with ALL the collateral damage that occurs with it.

Everyone's response to trauma is different and you're doing the best that you can with the capacity that is available to you and collectively as a family. There isn't a handbook for parents detailing the daily life of living with PTSD. Sure, you can go to a therapist, workshops, and more, but the challenge is feeling safe trusting anyone. And even as a couple, we were isolating from each other because we each needed to be able to survive. We each needed our own sanctuary to deal with it.

When things got very heavy, I would go for long drives, sit in parking lots, and just let the tears rolls down my cheeks in silence and hopelessness. I can't tell you how many times I considered driving off a mountain road or thought about crashing at high-speed into something to end it all. Ultimately, thoughts of my children or an unexpected police officer parked at the location I was considering would stop my thought, at that moment. However, my internal perpetrator was constantly feeding on my hopelessness.

Flawed Thinking

It took my daughter's trauma for me to realize I had thoughts and behaviors I needed to UNLEARN, release, and interrupt.

The habits I had created in my life fed my internal perpetrator and left me disconnected from my heart and soul. My brain was trying to keep me safe, but it had flawed thinking. What does that mean? Flawed thinking is driven by beliefs and negative tapes that aren't true. They run automatically in our heads and dictate self-sabotaging behaviors.

Flawed thinking often expresses our pain in a destructive way because we do not know how to communicate about the pain. Think about a time you have gotten angry about something, judged others, blown up, or acted out rebelliously. These are pain statements being acted out instead of saying the truth. I hurt. I feel worthless, not valued, confused about who I am, alone, abandoned, unsupported, or unloved. In our mind, we are protecting ourselves and staying out of our heart. We may not know what our truth is.

The voice of my truth was buried deep in that vault with my emotions. I didn't speak my truth. I was taught growing up with my mom that I was not to be emotional. She hated it when I was emotional. She'd tell me to fix my face! My mom's rules were not her; they were about her pain that she couldn't voice. I learned and lived those rules by putting my voice and truth into the vault to keep me safe. It wasn't safe to speak my truth.

When my daughter was victimized, I couldn't share the truth of how utterly broken I felt. How my heart hurt so bad that I didn't want to live any more. I felt so alone, and I wanted to die. My internal perpetrator fed on those feelings, jabbing at me every day about how worthless and disgusting I was. It made me believe no one would really want to be close friends with me; that I'm more valuable dead than alive. I kept hearing the negative tapes of my mother, wondering if I would ever be successful. Hearing her sounds of disgust when I didn't do it her way. Her behavioral confirmations that I was worthless. My internal perpetrator said my mom was right and continued to amplify the chanting negativity.

The Enabler in Me

So, how did I respond as a secondary survivor with my flawed thinking? I became an enabler without even knowing it. I acted from my own fears to protect my mind and safety while thinking my actions were helping my daughter. I just wanted our daughter to be safe and STAY alive.

Living with someone who has Post Traumatic Stress Disorder (PTSD) or more specifically, Complex PTSD can create a very chaotic life. You never know what each day is going to look like and what might trigger the survivor.

My daughter had extreme anxiety and feared for her life, resulting in her acting out her pain and feelings of worthlessness. Her perpetrator had made her believe it was her fault, and that SHE was the bad one. She told us that she was just damaged goods and that there is nothing she could do to change it. She couldn't speak about what happened with her, she couldn't even say her perpetrator's name. She was now a teenager living through the scared eyes of an 8-year-old child that just wanted to feel safe.

I wanted to hold that scared little girl and make the pain go away—and didn't know how. To compensate, I tried to do things for my daughter that might make her feel better, feel safe. I was so concerned about keeping her alive that I didn't have her keep up with her chores or do things that I normally would have. Yet, she was making choices that were not the best for her. She hung out with the wrong people, she started ditching school, and at times, she even put herself in danger by being out late walking in unsafe areas. She had her own flawed thinking.

Being an enabler does a huge disservice to yourself and to your loved one. I was basically sending my daughter the message that I didn't trust her to be able to do it herself. Did I know that at the time? No. I was focused on ME and what helped me feel safe. I didn't want my daughter to get hurt again or hurt herself. And then, she would do something that wasn't good for her, or for her future, and it would affirm my fears. I loved my daughter so much and was so scared. So, without knowing, I would enable her again. Enabling isn't about the person you're helping; enabling is about your own fears.

Being a rescuer, another name for enabler in this type of situation, takes the quick action of swooping in and taking over. And that's what I did. I didn't give my daughter enough time to feel her own consequences or apply my own consequences in response to her actions. I took on the responsibilities and did the work. I cleaned up the messes. I paid for things. And here's the sad part that I'm not proud of; I took ownership of her life. I usurped her personal power. I unintentionally affirmed her self-doubt because of my own fears. I didn't know I was doing all of this because I was flat out scared. My awareness of my behavior didn't come until later. Until I gained that awareness, this enabling/being enabled behavior became a wicked hamster wheel that kept going and going until we both ultimately started feeling resentful toward each other. We both were self-sabotaging and stuck.

Another part of me was stuck being unable to remove my mask. I grew up with a mask on. What saved me as a child was now smothering me as an adult. I was compartmentalizing my life, living on autopilot, and placing my emotions and brokenness into the vault to act as if I'm okay; even though I was dying inside.

"An unacknowledged trauma is like a wound that never heals over and may start to bleed again at any time."

~ALICE MILLER

DYING MOMENTS

Life as a secondary survivor is filled with a lot of grief because of all the "deaths" that occur. There are three areas of death that come to mind, 1) the death of the former life and all that was good, 2) the death of healthy boundaries, and 3) the reality of facing death.

The day we found out about our daughter's abuse is the day that our life shattered into pieces. There simply are not enough words to describe all that you experience and how you become untethered by the sheer knowledge that something traumatic has happened in your own life. And let's be honest, it takes time to reveal just how much you have been untethered.

Our family was having fun living life. We lived in the mountains west of Denver, Colorado and thought it was like living a dream. I would get up early and look out our windows just to take it all in. I had to keep telling myself that we lived here; this isn't just a vacation. We were surrounded by beauty. We had elk, deer, foxes, and sometimes an occasional mountain lion or raspberry stealer (a bear) honor us with their presence.

When we first bought this house, we didn't have a lot of furniture yet, so we played a game of laser tag in our empty house. My husband and I each wore the chest gear displaying the target, and our son and daughter carried the laser guns. We teamed up and took off running, jumping, dodging, screaming, and laughing all over the house. I even had to call a time out because I couldn't catch my breath from all of the running. We also played truth or dare to see if we individually could go sit on the swing in our night filled backyard for a count of 30. These were the things we were doing together. We enjoyed the normal everyday life of a family, school, work, chores, normal struggles, and family time. We were happy. We loved where we lived, and life was good. We all had dreams we wanted to fulfill.

When we found out our daughter had been a victim, the initial confusion, disbelief, and grief were intense. And then, the waves of mental and emotional anguish came crashing in again and again. I tried to get my bearings, but I couldn't. I struggled to see where I was and what I could safely grab on to. Just like losing a loved one, I missed our precious life of who we were as a family. I missed it, deeply. I cried for it, and I was heartbroken. Parts of me died with the news of the trauma. My trust died. My safety died. My dreams died.

Most of the time I kept to myself, stayed home, and dreaded gatherings. It is hard to gather with people and see their lives continue to move forward when you feel trapped in trauma. My brain kept trying to find out what happened and how I could've stopped it. I watched how people behaved, watched what they did. I looked at the innocence of the children in the room and ached for my own children's happiness to return. I couldn't talk about it. I didn't want to talk about it. I didn't know who to trust and so I isolated my thoughts and feelings about our life.

There were other parts of me that went numb and stopped living. I was in survival mode, and on autopilot. I learned to get up every day and do the basic things of getting my children to school and getting to work. I got very, very good at compartmentalizing my life and showing up as if nothing had happened.

Death of Boundaries

There's a saying, "If you don't stand for something, you'll fall for everything." I bring this up because when you have your feet knocked out from under you, there are a lot of boundaries that get wiped out too. One of the most basic boundaries that got wiped out for us was self-care. We lacked sleep, activities of self-care, and even day-to-day habits. Our family dinners stopped happening regularly. There were many nights I ate standing up at the kitchen counter because I didn't know what the evening would hold. Health care appointments got dropped or were not even scheduled for any of us. Sad to say, but everything came in at the same volume, and it was hard to decipher the important items or even remember things.

My hardest struggle since the trauma is to remember dates, times and other information. When writing this book, one of the challenges our family struggled with was identifying the year we found out about the abuse. Trauma obliterates parts of your memory and each of us holds different pieces, and yet, they never make a complete picture. It's like I somehow connect it to the event. I can remember the date, the looks, the visceral experience of that day, but I am hard pressed to remember a lot of things after that. I've learned to utilize tools to help me. I use my calendar and phone to implement reminders, create documentation, and set alerts.

I believe boundaries come with their own learning curve and when you add trauma to the mix, they become even more challenging to navigate. In fact, I would say that many boundaries get replaced with walls. Your life becomes focused on safety and protection. Keep people out and protect your heart. Our big, beautiful home shifted from a place that welcomed friends over frequently to a fortress to keep people out. Certain occasions, holidays, and traditions helped keep some of the normalcy in our lives, but the act of socially engaging went way down, which was hard. I'm an extrovert so connecting with people feeds me. Over time, I made sure I could do it safely. I was starting my coaching business, so I joined the local chamber of commerce. In 2007, I started volunteering with the chamber because it gave me a safe and easy way to connect without bringing it into my personal life. I got very involved in the business community.

I was out of the house a lot networking and building my business. This was a part of my life I absolutely loved, the part where I didn't have to feel the pain I felt when I walked into our home. Business was a great distraction for me. I was consistently exercising my business muscle and it was getting stronger and stronger. I was creating safe connections and enjoyed being able to support others in their dreams.

In my personal life, I wasn't exercising any boundaries and felt all over the place. I lived in guilt, shame, and exhaustion, never feeling like I was good enough. It was like seeing a body builder who has a massive upper body and toothpicks for legs. I was actively engaged in one area of my life and not exercising equal commitment in the other areas of my life. By achieving and experiencing success, I built my belief that I could at least contribute something good to the world. Not a bad intention; just an imbalanced one since I was covertly self-sacrificing by giving a part of myself away more and more. I was losing myself.

Facing the Reality of Death

Loss is the main ingredient to trauma. My daughter was getting more and more lost as her anxiety grew. I cannot know, or even guess, her thoughts as she navigated her own deep betrayal and abuse. Therapists working with my husband and me would tell us we were lucky she was still functional with day-to-day things. We were lucky that she wasn't addicted to alcohol or drugs. Each time we went to the hospital or an emergency mental health clinic, the same questions occurred. What happened? Is she addicted to any drugs or alcohol? No. Well, get her into more therapy.

My daughter was so tired of always starting at square one and without being given the tools and support that showed her how to move forward from where she was in life right now. We always started with square one: What happened? And are you addicted to drugs or alcohol? They would test to see if she had anything in her system. No. She just felt unsafe with herself and wanted the pain to stop. At one of the hospital visits, the therapist stated that they couldn't enroll her because she did not have any addictions and was not, in this moment, actively trying to kill herself. I asked the therapist, "You mean she has to slit her wrist or do something to risk her life before she gets any type of support or help?!"

Basically, yes. These were the type of responses and "support" we would receive again and again. And even when we looked at private programs to enroll her in, the cost was over $25,000 for one month. We were barely hanging onto our house by this point. How would we be able to take on this expense as well. We wouldn't even qualify for it!

There was one specific suicide ideation we had at the hospital when she was overwhelmed with despair and felt completely hopeless. I was running home to grab something, and my husband called me. He said we need to prepare ourselves because she might not come out of this alive. I knew it. I could feel it. I was stunned into silence. I just drove in the thick silence that was enveloping me. There were no words… to this day there are still no words, just tears.

When I look back, what I have learned over the years is that there was still an addiction that occurred. Recently, during the writing of this book, I discovered research has come out about behavioral addiction. "The specific impact of a childhood trauma is nuanced and complex, yet one common outcome is the dysregulation of the stress system. (Burke Harris, 2018; Moustafa et al., 2021)" [4]

This is the addiction we felt our daughter had; it seemed she had a behavioral addiction to chaos. If life became too smooth or something good came about, she would be okay for a few days or even a couple of weeks. Then she would do something to pick a fight with us and start yelling or raging. Other times she would do something that sabotaged her efforts to move forward. For example, she dropped out of school on the first day of her senior year. She turned down an opportunity to play soccer abroad—she quit.

She was stuck in the cycle of ups and downs; like riding an extreme rollercoaster. She didn't know how to get off the ride. Her brain was saying good never lasts long, just like her childhood. She'd be safe until the next time she saw her perpetrator. It was like her brain was telling her danger was just around the corner—be prepared. She was so used to being in survival mode, protecting herself that she didn't know how to stay in a place of enjoyment. She didn't know how to express her feelings. The most frequent response we saw from her was numbness. She didn't cry. And when she did express emotions, it was usually rage. We didn't have an

---

4   Giordano 2021

understanding or resource at the time, but I am very glad the knowledge exists today.

As I was losing myself, the threat of losing my daughter was simultaneously intensifying. I cannot tell you how many sleepless nights and suicide ideations we went through. Harrowing moments. I had my small group or "council" of friends that I trusted and still didn't open up to them as much as I needed or wanted to. Security was a nonnegotiable for me and being vulnerable was too risky. Hence why my healing has taken so long. I wasn't willing to be vulnerable and risk my own heart. And yet, that's where healing needs to take place. The biggest damage had occurred in my heart, and yet I wasn't willing to be vulnerable and risk admitting it needed repair. Fear ran my decisions at the time, and I didn't think there was any other way.

I want you to understand this fear because this is where people get stuck in their healing. When you're betrayed at such a deep level you don't know where or who to turn to, you isolate and try to do it all by yourself. Yes, I had some counseling but struggled with my own trust within that space. I had this fearful perspective that if I told someone all that I was feeling then somehow it would completely empty me, leaving nothing but a husk that would drop over and die.

As a young woman my first experience with therapy was with our church minister. Unfortunately, right before one of my sessions, he told me that he had just gotten off the phone with my mom. She was the reason I was going to therapy and was great at gaining information from people who I considered to be of support to me. I knew how she worked, so I immediately stood up and walked out of the office never to return for therapy at the church.

As I have said before, what is unhealed within us gets magnified. The betrayals in my life and their effects were increasingly compounding, putting me at dangerously high levels of mental and emotional pain that were overpowering my ability to survive. I started to think about suicide. I grew up with the belief that suicide is a sin, so I prayed every night for God to take me. I prayed, cried, begged for God to take me and stop the suffering. Nothing. I started to look at ways to end my life. I would be driving down the canyon and see a place on the road that didn't have as many barriers and thought about speeding up and going full speed off the edge. I was contemplating different plans.

One day I drove to work and was really struggling. I worked with a great staff, and I talked to a colleague that day, but I couldn't get over the intense feeling of helplessness. I don't even remember our conversation. What I do remember was at the end of the workday, I got in my car and decided that I was going to kill myself. I couldn't live this way anymore.

I drove home crying. Once I got home, I proceeded to search for my husband's handgun. I held it in my hand and looked at it, read the serial number. Then I wrote my letter and put it under my pillow. There was a huge mirror on the floor that was waiting to be installed, I sat in front of it and looked at myself holding the gun. I started to cry. I didn't want to die. I just couldn't bear the pain anymore and I couldn't figure out how to stop it. The intense hopelessness and pain felt like it was consuming me. I held the gun near my head, then thought about holding the gun to my heart. I so desperately wanted to stop the pain in both places and didn't know how to do it simultaneously. I cried to God to help me—and a quick vision popped into my head. A vision of my son coming home from school with his coat and backpack on and entering the house. He would be the first one to find me. I cried again. I put the gun down and put it away.

My mind buzzing, I felt enveloped by a thickness I can't describe. Later, after my son got home, I drove him to his class in east Denver. It would take a while to get there since we lived in the mountains to the west. I remember that day we saw a bear sitting on the side of the hill as we were returning home. All the cars on the road, in both directions, had pulled over to see the bear. I did too. My son got to see the bear while I sat in the thickness of my grief. I don't recall anything else from that day.

The next day I felt regret for not ending my life because the pain was more intense. I got up from bed later during the night, headed to the back hall, thinking about it again. My husband came searching for me. I don't know what all happened, whether my husband got notified by my coworker or what, but he was checking in on me and my whereabouts. At some point around this time, my sister-in-law showed up at our home. She was there to be with me. We had grown up as best friends, but our relationship had changed a lot over the years, and we weren't as close. Having her show up at my home and show her support was like a ray of light coming into my life. I admitted to her I was afraid to go to therapy because I was scared once I let everything out that I would just be empty and drop over dead. She assured me that I would fill up with good things that would replace the bad.

You'd think I would have gone to therapy if death was the outcome I was suspecting. Like I said, I didn't really want to die, I just wanted the pain to stop. I wish we could ask people who have crossed over from suicide whether they really wanted to die or if they just wanted the pain to stop. That's what I wanted. I wanted my heart and mind to stop hurting so intensely. I wanted the hopelessness to go away. I wanted to believe that my life could be different. For now, I made a commitment to my husband to take it day-to-day and to get into therapy again.

*"The moment you accept responsibility
for everything in your life
is the moment you gain the power
to change anything in your life."*

—HAL ELROD

GETTING OFF THE RIDE

My husband and I got married in 1988. I couldn't have found a better man. He has such wisdom, humor, intensity, and love for our family. I'm not sure if I could've survived this storm without him. The one thing we truly focused on was striving to keep our daughter alive and let her know we loved her no matter what. We knew that these tragedies could break up marriages and families. With our daughter being an at-risk-youth, we didn't want her to feel she was at fault for breaking up our marriage. So, my husband and I decided to extend the same belief to each other—that we loved each other no matter what.

Couples going through secondary survivorship test the very existence of themselves and their relationship. There are times you're angry, weak, apathetic, depressed, and more—capacity runs low, while frustrations run high. There are various levels of connection and disconnection. That's how my son got sucked up into this storm. We focused so much on our daughter's survival that he felt left behind, neglected. Did we realize it at the time? No. We thought we were protecting him, too. Keeping him out of harm's way, but instead, the message he inadvertently was receiving from both of us was that he wasn't important enough to have our attention.

No matter how much you love your children and spouse, you're going to make mistakes. There is going to be collateral damage that is unforeseen, and you will need to face it. At some point, to start the healing, you will have to face truths you didn't know existed. I felt so ashamed and deeply hurt that my son felt neglected. I didn't want to hear that he felt neglected. I didn't want to feel that shame. I love our son more than words can express. His truth is from his experience. We can't negate that. We can't wave it away and say, "You just don't understand."

The point is, that was his experience, his truth. And instead of resisting it, I must face my part in it. There are parts of my son's life that were negatively impacted because of what was happening in our house, times he won't get back. There were times that he needed us too and we weren't there. What was happening in our communication with each other? What was happening from our own fears? He had his own secondary trauma experience from our trauma and fears. My words of apology will never be enough for my son, my love in my actions is what helps to bring healing individually and collectively. Truth prevails and we can either face the truth and mend it, or we can ignore it and allow the damage and suffering to continue.

A Choice

"Suffering is a choice."

I remember seeing that headline of an article in our local newspaper. Just reading the title alone made me angry. How dare they! WTF?! I was so angry! I couldn't believe someone would say something like that. The article was written by a local psychotherapist who understood trauma. He discussed the mind and how it can make us believe that we don't have a choice. He went on to explain that we do have a choice.

We cannot control what happens to us, but we can control how we respond to it which inevitably leads to suffering or healing.

I had to sit with it. Let it sink in because I was still resisting the title so strongly. I had been triggered by it.

I got angry! I finally got angry with God too! I had attended church every Sunday. Read the Bible. Did what a good little girl would do and toed the (unbearable) line that my mom had drawn for me and my life. I did everything I possibly could do to be "perfect" in my behavior. I didn't break the rules, I didn't talk back. I fulfilled my responsibilities. I was vigilantly focused on good behavior. However, this newspaper article brought up rage I hadn't accessed before. I got pissed. I didn't understand this thought about suffering being a choice. I felt damned by God. I had worked at the very church that my daughter's perpetrator was active in. And now you're going to tell me suffering was a choice!! I had to get out of there. I had to take a drive…a long one at that.

I questioned everything about God and "his" existence. What proof do I have? Who is this big God that decides whether you go to heaven or hell?! Damn YOU, God! Damn YOU! We are good people and look what you let happen to us! I never understood the concept of heaven and hell. If God is our loving father than how is it that he would ever choose to put a child in hell? I love my daughter, and she made some horrific choices after surviving her abuse and I still wouldn't put her in hell. I would continue to love-on her, to show her, to teach her, to never give up on her. I was angry and had to keep driving. I was going to drive my way to the truth.

Once I finally vented all that I needed to, which admittedly, was a lot, I began to relax and take in the view. I just kept driving in the silence. Then all of a sudden, a different scenario came into my mind. I said, "Wait a minute!! I'm being shown what heaven or hell is right now! I've been in hell. I've made decisions that keep me in pain. I have a choice! Right now! I can either choose to live in heaven or live in hell. I can do this differently."

The beliefs I grew up with drastically changed during that drive. I no longer saw myself as a sinner. I saw myself the same way I saw my two children when they were born. Pure love. Perfect. Love in action. I didn't see them as humans that had to be saved. I saw them as precious lives to be loved. Did life get in the way of happiness? Yes, but it doesn't have to be forever! I had to understand that this pain did not have to exist forever at the intensity that it did. I understood the article, now. Life delivered the unexpected and the choices I made were in response to what happened to our daughter—I was choosing more pain, more isolation, and more hopelessness.

In that moment, I realized, for me, churches kept God and our thinking very small. I felt like churches were teaching what the Pharisees believed instead of what Jesus walked, lived, and taught. Jesus met people where they were at in life and loved them no matter what. He shared parables to help people understand how to make good choices in life. I'm not here to change your beliefs. I am here to tell you that your faith and any beliefs you have are going to be challenged. Some will fall away, new ones will emerge, others will strengthen, and you will start to piece together the things in your life that make sense, bring back hope. I believe these renewed beliefs will empower you with love, healing, and the very essence of heaven on earth.

When my own choices for living in hell came to my awareness, I started to really pay attention to my thoughts and actions. I knew I could learn to look at and question things differently. I didn't need to be scared. I needed to be empowered. And what I learned was that I was on an emotional ride with my daughter. One that was scary and unpredictable.

How did I know I was on the ride with her? Simple, I started checking in with myself to see if when she was feeling up; I was too. If she was feeling down; I was down. My experiences were mirroring her moods; that's when I realized I was on the ride! You can do the same thing to see if you're riding someone else's emotional rollercoaster. You can check to see if you're up when they're up and if you're down when they're down; then you're on the ride my friend. You need to get off the emotional ride.

Here's why this is so important. When you get off the ride you create an exit path for them to do the same by modeling behaviors of boundaries, self-care, and self-love. Whether you feel like they are taking it in or not; they are. Imagine yourself getting on a rollercoaster with your loved one only to be stuck feeling all that they feel. It's their ride, they own it, and you don't get to stop it when you want to. They are in control, and you are at their beck and call.

Now, imagine yourself in a different position, you are standing by or sitting on a park bench waiting for them outside of the ride. They can see you; they know you are there, but you're not having to experience their ride minute-by-minute. You have some distance and observe the ride that they're on. You're able to respond differently because your perspective comes from a different position. They get to choose to stop and get off their ride or to keep going. And that's a powerful difference.

When I was on that emotional ride with my daughter; I was enabling her. When I learned to get off the ride, I was able to model healthy choices that she could make as well. The choice and practice of getting off the ride was NOT easy or comfortable, but I've learned that change and growth live outside our comfort. The work isn't easy; it's powerful. Life started shifting for me as my awareness of being on the ride or off it increased.

There is a definite learning curve because it's easy to fall back into old patterns. Be patient with yourself, it starts with identifying where you are. Allow the new learning to strengthen while the old patterns weaken. Unlearning is challenging and it takes awareness, practice, and time to shift positions. You don't always have to analyze things. Sometimes you just need to release or interrupt those patterns to help you stay off the ride.

When my daughter got off the ride she was in a healthier place. However, it wasn't always easy to spot when she got back on. She would start sharing what she was going through and then all of a sudden, bam! I would find myself back on the ride. She's up; I'm up. She's down; I'm down. Damn it! That's when I started identifying this behavior as emotional tickets to the ride. We've all bought at least one (or one million) in our lives. The tendency is to want to relieve a person's current pain and without knowing it, we may find ourselves more involved than we wanted to be. We get entangled in the emotions and don't know what to do. Well, check-in, see if you're on the ride. Getting off the ride is a powerful practice. The learning typically starts with hindsight, and then you start to see where you've purchased your emotional tickets in the past so that you can identify the emotional triggers more and more. They're like little cries for help but it's not about helping them get out of it; it's a cry to get into the feelings with them, into the drama.

When I sense or see an emotional ticket now, I have to ask myself. Is this my responsibility? Is this mine to solve, to mend, or to clean up? If not, then I am empathetic and can choose to be a supportive observer or remove myself from the scene. Tough love. Not easy; powerful.

Getting off the ride requires mental tools and strategies to help guide and support you. A mantra I am currently practicing in my life when emotional situations or triggers come up for me is to say, "I am a rock, and rocks don't pick up messes." A rock is supportive, strong, quiet, and listens. I remind myself that the person is capable, and I can mentor instead of rescue. I can learn to customize my support.

"Support is not something you find; it's something you create."

—CHRIS HADFIELD

CUSTOMIZING SUPPORT

I was suffocating in our home with our story, and I wanted it to stop. I told my husband that I was going to go over to our neighbors and ask them if they could come up for a talk. I just wanted to be able share what we'd been going through for years with SOMEONE! My husband was fearful of this approach. He wasn't sure and thought it would be too vulnerable, that we'd be judged, and in the end, it would come back to hurt us. I explained, I couldn't live another day like this. I needed someone around us to know.

Our neighbors came over. They sat down on our couch as I shared some things that we were going through. I explained all that we were experiencing and if they had seen the police at our house, it is because of our daughter, her experience, and her choices. I just wanted someone to know. When we finished sharing our story, we looked at them. They sat there silent and stunned. After a while the husband said he didn't even know how to respond. He didn't know. As they got up to leave, they offered their support to us. I finally felt some of the weight of the world leave my shoulders. I could breathe deeper. I felt freer and more importantly, felt hope. Someone knew.

This single act of truly reaching out and being vulnerable created a crack in my mask that let the light in. I became hungry for it. I started to mention to people that my daughter was an at-risk-youth, and we were navigating this in our lives. I served on the Parent-Teacher council at the high school, and we were planning an education night on parenting teenagers. The chairwoman expressed that she knew we were going through something with our daughter and wondered if I would be willing to say something the night of the event. I told her I would like to share our story and ask my husband to be part of the talk as well. I felt the audience would be better served hearing from both parents. I went home and asked my husband. He was in. After we wrote our talking points, we shared them with each other and then our daughter. We wanted her to know what we were sharing and if she was okay with it. She said, "Wow, I've been a good teacher." Yes, you have. A painful teacher...and a powerful one too.

The night of the event, I sat down and prayed for guidance. I wanted my words to help others. I also wanted to share my truth and say what I needed to say. Our talk was structured in two parts to open and close the event. The first portion focused on the dark side, our daughter's behaviors, and our own family struggles, then the audience went to break out sessions for about 90-minutes. The second half of our talk was about the light and hope in our situation. My husband and I spoke about our commitment to each other and the power of loving unconditionally. We also shared a few tools and our approaches to our situation.

The audience filled an entire side of the gym and the biggest fear I had before our talk was having hundreds of people come up to me and say, "You know what you should do...." We got that all the time, as if they were the experts on our family. It never helped and it never felt supportive. So, the one thing I *had* to say to the audience was, "I know you're sitting there thinking of the many things you think we should do. But before you do; I want you to know all of the things we have done and have tried in order to help our daughter." And then I went down our very long list of approaches, experts, nutrition, meds, therapies, etc. By the end of my list, you heard the gasp from the audience acknowledging that we had tried everything possible to shift what was happening in our lives.

After we were done closing the event, we stepped to the side of the gymnasium so the breakout session leaders could be acknowledged. What happened next was so amazing. People were coming down from the bleachers and lining up in front of my husband and me. Some were giving us accolades for being so brave in sharing our story, friends tearfully came up saying they never knew we were in pain because we hid it so well. And still others were lining up to share their own personal pain and stories and asking for guidance. I felt such relief and connection. It felt so good to be able to help people look at their own situations differently. We gave tools and resources where we could in the short time that we had.

Later we got calls from the school principal to see if we would be willing to connect and talk with parents that were struggling with their own children. We held workshops at the high school and local human services center so parents could find some true support. I still teach my clients these tools and even have them calling me after our work together when tragedy has struck. They know I am understanding, compassionate, and most importantly have tools that they can use to get back on their feet.

Our driving point, at the time of our talk, was that your child or loved one is in charge of their choices. As parents, family, or friends, you might wish you were in charge; but you're not. Ultimately your best options are to prepare multiple game plans to respond to their choices, provide unconditional love, and customize your support.

While we're on the topic of choices, I want to add something here that I feel is very important. Don't force your children to hug adults. Let them choose. Children have their own sense of safety when they're little and if they don't feel like hugging the adult then honor their decision. I don't care who the adult is, friend, acquaintance, family member, or neighbor. Let your child choose whether they want to hug them or not so they can start listening to their own internal alarms.

Ok, onward to ways we can customize our support.

Game Plans

My daughter, as a teenager, acted out a lot and on one of my "watches" she ran away. Damn it! Our protocol was to call the police. At this time, I was still learning not to be an enabler, so of course, my fears showed up first. I knew I was to make the call, but I was resisting hard. I had given my word to my husband and still was struggling to make the call. So, I started thinking—game plan, what's my game plan? I need help.

I picked up our phone and called my neighbor. I asked her if she had a moment to talk and said, "Okay, I'm going to ask you something, and after I'm done explaining what I need, you have full permission to tell me no. I need you to come up to my house. Just walk in. I'm in the kitchen. My daughter has run away, and I need to call the police to report her as a runaway. Can you please just walk into my house, stand silently in the kitchen until you hear me call the police. Once my phone call is done can you just leave?"

She agreed to do EXACTLY what I asked for. She came into the house and just stood there and waited. I was vacillating again, so I called a friend who had an at-risk son, she confirmed that, yes, I needed to call the police, so I finally made the call. I hung up the phone and looked at my neighbor. She nodded her head toward me and quietly asked, "Are you good?" Yes. And then she quietly departed and never brought up the incident again. This is what I needed. I needed someone to be there for ME; not to rescue me, not to be the expert over me, just be there to support me in a crisis.

People truly believe that they'll know how to support others but that isn't always true. They may not know what you need and so they guess what will work for you. Instead, you are going to have to learn how to get what you need by customizing your support. Ask, specifically, for what you need. I didn't need my neighbor to make the call for me; I needed someone to silently stand by me, to hold me accountable for a task that needed to be done. This helped to empower me. I was able to overcome the emotional difficulty of the tasks because I had support literally standing by. You can do the same. Start asking yourself what you truly need and get specific when asking for it. This was a game changer in my life.

Mindset Trumps Strategy

Your mindset is your biggest tool since everything starts with thought. One thing I frequently share is that mindset trumps strategy. I'll say it again. Mindset trumps strategy. You can have the best laid out plans but if your mindset is not aligned you will default to your beliefs. I have seen people try to affirm their way out of a hole by saying between 5 to 20, or more, affirmations and yet experience no change. It's the same with prosperity. A person can say affirmations to try and create or manifest money but if their belief is that nothing is really going to change then your mindset has trumped your strategy of reciting affirmations.

Your core pictures or beliefs are where your thoughts come from. Your external reflects your internal. I could always tell when my daughter wasn't doing well because her room was a mess, and her behavior was off. Same with me, I wanted to get out of pain, but my mindset was saying we were stuck in hell, and I was a horrible mother. Hard to get out of a hole when you're using a shovel to dig deeper.

When you find yourself feeling worse, feeling the pain. pause for a moment and take a deep breath. Your brain is either working in the past or in the future and we need it to be in the present moment. Get into the now. Take some deep breaths until you feel grounded. Ask yourself, "What do I want?" So many times, we're trying to avoid what we don't want, and we keep focusing on that instead of what we want. Once you get clear on what you want, then ask yourself what needs to happen to make that possible? Take a baby step of identifying the next thing you can do to get closer to what you want—even if it's a tiny step.

For example, my brain would be worrying about my daughter's future and what she needed to do to get to a better life. I was living in the future. I would stop myself, breathe, and confirm that my daughter was safe and okay right here—right now. Then I could ask myself what can I do to be of support? What can I let go of that stops me from being present with my daughter? I was learning to be more present with myself and my daughter.

The Doubt Tool

I used to call my husband Doubting Thomas because any new idea I brought up or he contemplated would be filled with doubts. Yet he would generate opportunities time and time again. It would drive me crazy! I finally asked him what he was doing. How did he create opportunities when he was doubting everything? He said he used doubt differently and that it would be hard to explain. After a few months, he finally shared how he uses doubt to his benefit. I have since translated it into my own tool for how I use doubt and teach my clients how to use it as well.

Think of your third eye, or the center of your forehead, as your decision-maker. You only get to have one belief hold this position as you make a decision. Whenever we try to stretch ourselves, or do something new, we tend to doubt ourselves. Most people fall back into the comfort of what's familiar and don't move forward. Here's what you can do differently. The next time you are doubting yourself, I want you to stop and ask which two beliefs are battling to be the decision-maker? Typically, you will find that a new belief is emerging, and the old belief is trying to keep you safe. It's battling for position.

For example, when I first started writing this book, I had a ton of doubt. In fact, I walked into my husband's room and said, "I wish I was a quitter because I just want to quit. Who's going to buy this book anyway." After we chatted for a bit, I realized I had two beliefs trying to battle for position of decision-maker. Do I stay with the familiarity of not writing a book and quit? Or do I let the new belief emerge that I can be a published author and keep writing? Which one serves my highest good? I got back in my office and kept writing.

When you are doubting yourself on how to navigate life as a secondary survivor, it will serve you to revisit your beliefs when doubt comes up. Life has changed and with it will be new beliefs that can help you move forward. They may be unfamiliar but if you don't practice working with the new belief then you will stay where it is safe and comfortable. I didn't say pain-free, as secondary survivors we've learned the chaos can feel safe and comfortable because we've lived with its familiarity.

Salt Moments

I don't know about you but when we make mistakes, we tend to punish ourselves. I remember a time when my son was young, and it was his responsibility to get his dance bag ready for his competition the next day. We'd have to leave early. We checked with him to see if it was packed. He said yes. We had placed a condition that if his bag was not ready, we wouldn't be attending the competition. This wasn't a team competition; it was solo. The next morning, we were loading the car when we saw him standing at the top of the stairs, fully dressed, except for one shoe. Where's your shoe? He didn't know. We started unpacking the car because that was the consequence of not having everything ready in his bag.

Later, I went up to talk to him. I said, sometimes we make mistakes, but we could use today's mistake to learn. I then defined what I call salt moments. Have you ever touched a cut with your hands and felt it sting because of the oils and dirt on our hands? The sting would be even worse if we rubbed salt into the cut. Instead of using salt to cause pain and thinking of it as a failure; think of it as a way to learn.

I proceeded to explain how we use salt to enhance the flavor of cooking and how great it can be. I wanted him to take just enough salt from today's incident and learn how to enhance his life in a better way. Carol Dweck, the author of *Mindset, The New Psychology for Success* explains it as two mindsets. A fixed mindset and a growth mindset. We each possess both mindsets dependent on the situation and life experience. The fixed mindset feels almost like you have pigeon-holed yourself to a certain station in life. You don't risk failure therefore you don't risk a lot of growth. A person with a growth mindset understands that they can learn from their mistakes hence they are willing to take risks. Read her book. It's a good one.

When you are surviving trauma, your mind can be all over the place. For me, I wasn't taking any risks. I was stuck in some serious fixed mindset and rubbing tons of salt into my wounds.

Salt moments are about choosing. When you make a mistake do you rub criticism and judgment into your wound and make it worse, or do you step back and take what you need from it so you can enhance and improve your life. Oh, and I get it, sometimes the mistakes are so bad that you have a ton of salt that has spilled all over everything. Be gentle with yourself. You're human. Give yourself space to recover then go shake off the salt, pick up the lesson, and learn from it. Embracing the learning will empower you to move forward.

Tag Team

My husband and I started strategizing our responses as a team approach. We started to check-in with each other every day to see who had the capacity if our daughter were to call one of us. If I had the capacity and my husband didn't, I would answer her call, and he wouldn't. Then we would shift responsibility if the capacity was reversed. This helped us maintain a better level of capacity and communication each day.

We also created subtle physical signals we would give each other to call a time out when dealing with our daughter. I might step a certain way or cross in front of my husband, he would signal with his hand so that we both knew to look at each other and call a time out with our daughter. We used the signals when our daughter had hit a spot where my husband and I were no longer on the same page, and it had the potential to divide and conquer us. We would pause, tell our daughter to sit there while we go talk for a bit. We'd leave the room, and debate or talk out the topic. Once we reached consensus, we'd head back to our daughter. A united front helped these situations. If we, as a couple, were divided, applying consequences to our daughter's choices would become even more difficult.

That's the real point that is being made. Kids don't purposely try to divide and conquer their parents. I think it's in our nature to do that. If there is an area of weakness, it becomes the target, which then becomes the distraction in the moment. My husband and I got very good at paying attention to whether we were united or divided. We became focused on strengthening our team approach, even to call in outside support, like the police, when needed.

The Balance of Yes and No

This is a simple tool if you tend to lack boundaries, self-sacrifice, or are a people pleaser. Whenever you are asked to do something, stop, and ask yourself who you are saying yes to and who you are saying no to. For example, let's say a friend asks you to go out with her but you don't feel like it. If you say yes to your friend, you are saying no to you which puts you out of balance. If you decline your friend's request with a no, then you are saying yes to what you want which puts you in alignment. Another alignment can be yes and yes, if you want to go out with your friend.

F1—F2

This next one is sort of like the "Balance of Yes and No," but it packs a punch. When trying to decide, if you're vacillating, I want you to ask yourself if it is a "Fuck Yes!" or "Fuck No!" Things get very clear when you ask this type of question.

A friend and I were attending a festival, and we stopped at a food truck. She was perusing the menu when I asked her if this was where she wanted to get lunch. She hemmed and hawed as I stood there waiting. I finally said, "It's either a Fuck Yes! or a Fuck No!" She looked at me, shocked, and started to laugh. She said, "Fuck no, that made it easy to decide." And then we went and found something we both really wanted to enjoy for lunch. These tools can be used for the simplest and toughest situations. Learn them, practice them, and learn how to navigate what life brings you.

I'll be honest with you, the F1 and F2 tool is one of my clients' favorites!

FEARS Strategies: When in Crisis

As my husband and I got stronger with our approach, we developed an acronym to help us. I use this tactic to this day with family, friends, and even teach this to my clients. When you are going through a crisis, you will want to follow the **FEARS** strategy. The acronym is used as five checkpoints that may be used once or be repeated again and again until you get clear of the crisis. Here are the checkpoints:

- **FOCUS ON THE FACT:** Many times, we focus on our emotions or our opinions. You must dig down and truly identify the FACT. When you think you've identified it, ask yourself, is this an opinion? If the answer is yes, you need to keep digging. If not, then move to the next step.

- **EMOTIONAL EFFICACY:** To produce a desired or intended result that best supports your emotional/mental fitness in this specific situation, acknowledge how you are feeling. Let yourself be angry, scared, sad, whatever emotion that comes up. Then move the emotion to the side so you can focus on the fact. You'll touch base with your feelings again at a different time. You can feel what you feel, acknowledge them, and then move them to the side so they do not overtake your decision-making.

- **ACCOUNTABILITY:** Who is accountable to the fact? If one of the people who is accountable is you, then proceed to the next checkpoint. If you're not directly responsible or accountable, then move to the SAFER strategies.

- **RESPONSE TO THE FACT:** You have identified that you are accountable to the fact, so, how do you want to respond to the fact? What actions will help create a solution? When you are done responding to the fact, then move to the final checkpoint.

- **SELF-CHECK:** Where are you now and what is the next step? Keep repeating the FEARS checkpoints until the situation has been resolved or cleared.

Let's walk through a scenario together to illustrate how we've used FEARS.

> **SCENARIO:** *The high school calls and informs me that our daughter is not in her class. Since my daughter was ditching school and running away at this age there were a lot of thoughts going through my head, so I moved into the FEARS checkpoints.*

F: FOCUS ON THE FACT: My daughter is not in class. First, here are examples of opinions I went through before identifying the FACT. She's ditching class again. She's run away with so-and-so. Do you see how my emotions could have taken over? I had to get to the FACT that my daughter was not in class and that's the only fact I knew at the time.

E: EMOTIONAL EFFICACY: I'm feeling emotional pain wondering what she's doing, I'm scared she's run away. I'm worried about her future and what she's going to do in life. I'm angry that she's putting us through this again. I'm exhausted. Okay, I've acknowledged my feelings. I am going to ask myself to set these emotions aside so I can be present in the NOW and focus on the one fact I know.

A: ACCOUNTABILITY: Who is accountable to the FACT that my daughter is not in class.

1. My daughter (but she's the one missing).

2. The school because it's their legal responsibility within school hours.

3. My husband and I because she is under the age of 18. Okay, I'm an accountable person.

R: RESPONSE TO THE FACT: So how do I want to respond to the fact that my daughter is missing? I called the school to ask them what they are doing to locate my daughter. I notify my husband, and I call friends who are also parents who might have seen my daughter out and about. I drive to the local hangout to see if my daughter has ditched school. And then I return home to see if there are any messages. The school calls and notifies me that my daughter had been pulled from class for a test before attendance was taken and the teacher hadn't been notified, hence the report of her not being in class.

S: SELF-CHECK: What is the current situation? How do I feel now? My daughter is in school safe and sound. My emotions could've really taken me down a bad road. I followed the check points and engaged in actions I deemed needed, and requested/required the other accountable people to do the same. There is no need to implement consequences because the fact showed a mistake was not made by my daughter. The school staff member gained a learning opportunity about increasing communication when taking a student prior to the bell.

The key to using the FEARS strategy is to make sure you are one of the people accountable to the situation at-hand.

Often, I see people getting into family fights when they are not accountable. They try to "carry" the other person's life and responsibility. I know it is uncomfortable to see a loved one struggle, but please know that there is power within the struggle. You must not rescue them from learning their own lessons and doing the mental and emotional work that will empower them.

SAFER Strategies: Supporting Others in Crisis

My husband and I understood that we also needed a tool that could help support other people. I took the same letters that spelled FEARS and rearranged them to create an acronym using the word SAFER. You will want to follow the **SAFER** strategy when you are NOT the one going through a crisis. This is a tool you can use to support others. The acronym is also used as FIVE checkpoints that may be used once or be repeated again and again until you get clear on the support to be given. Here are the checkpoints:

• SELF-CHECK: What is my intent for giving support? Am I trying to be the hero by trying to rescue everyone?

Am I trying to take control as "the expert?" Or do I want to find out how I can best support the people going through the pain?

- **ASK, ASK, ASK:** Ask questions about how you can be of support. Examples are: Do they need meals provided at this time? Do they need help with care for any children? Do they need help with getting to an appointment? If they don't have something to tell you at that time; then leave it be. Honor their choice of not asking for help. Check-in when you feel prompted to. If they do ask for help, then continue with the next checkpoint.

- **FOCUS ON THE ASK:** Stay very clear on the focus of what the person/family said they needed and do not tie any judgments to it. If they ask for a meal or ask you to just sit and be present in the house and not say anything, then you know what their ask is.

- **EMOTIONAL EQUILIBRIUM:** Check to make sure you have the emotional capacity to fulfill their need. If yes, continue. If not, be honest. When my daughter ran away, I had a couple of friends who didn't feel they could help and that's okay. It kind of stings at the time but don't judge them. They have their own work, life, and triggers. It is important that you know your own emotional capacity before stepping in to help others. Again, step in with love, not judgment. Judgment shuts people down. Love keeps them moving forward no matter how small the steps may seem.

- **RESPOND TO THE ASK:** If you have the capacity to do so, fulfill an ask. When complete, if you feel aligned, go through the SAFER strategies again and continue to offer support.

Let's walk through a scenario together to illustrate how I've used SAFER to support people in my life.

> SCENARIO: *A friend of mine was dealing with the end stages of cancer.*

S: SELF-CHECK: Why did I want to get involved? I wanted to see how I might be able to extend support to my friend during this difficult time.

A: ASK, ASK, ASK: I asked how I could best support her. She didn't have much of a response as she didn't want to burden me. Luckily, she had asked a closer friend for support, and a sign-up schedule was created to help fulfill specific needs.

F: FOCUS ON THE ASK: One of my friend's needs was meals following a specific criteria and delivery plan.

E: EMOTIONAL EQUILIBRIUM: I knew cooking wouldn't require a lot of emotional investment from me. The meal sign-up was the best way, for me, to provide support to my friend.

R: RESPOND TO THE ASK: I signed up on the meal schedule, at the intervals I could handle, while honoring my own emotional equilibrium.

Sometimes we want to help more than we are capable of or have the capacity to do so. I wanted to be of more help to my friend and I just couldn't muster the energy physically or emotionally. It was necessary to check-in with myself to see what capacity I had to help. I had learned to put boundaries around myself so I could maintain a healthy mental and emotional balance. What I found was that my friend also had many other friends who had the capacity to support her in the other ways that she needed. She was also a very private person so most of the people were family or very, very close friends.

It's about creating a community of customized support. My friend received the support she needed, and friends were able to engage at some level of support throughout her journey. It works for people who are very private, as well as those who are more open. We just need to ask what they need, and sometimes it has to come from their closest friends in order to maintain their privacy. Perfect. Allow them to be honored in that space.

These are just a few of the many tools I learned to put in my tool belt as a secondary survivor. I continue to use various tools myself and teach them to my clients, friends, and family. When you are a secondary survivor, you must learn to step deeper into life. I had to learn how to be even more of a parent because of my daughter. I had to learn how to respond with tough love; to learn to be a stronger version of myself at the soul level; and come from a place of love both for myself and for others. Funny thing is, that sometimes I show up better if I put my coaching hat on because there isn't judgment or worry. I choose better words. Other times I need to just be a mom and let my son or daughter vent knowing there is nothing for me to fix.

"Healing is a journey, an exploration of the soul. It requires patience, faith, and an unwavering belief in the power of divine grace."

—DEEPAK CHOPRA

THE EBB AND FLOW
OF HEALING

When I think of healing, I like to envision a river or a creek. I took a group of youth and chaperones to Bear Creek in Morrison, Colorado to share an analogy of life. I asked each youth and adult to go find a place along the banks to identify where they felt they were in their life. I wanted them to take it in, to observe the movement of the water, the rocks, and where they were in the landscape of the water.

Once they had some time to observe and think about it, we gathered as a group to talk about the places where we saw ourselves. One youth said he was the water behind a big rock; it kind of trapped things, and him, against the rock and was turbulent. Another said they were floating down the creek like the leaf. Another said she was pulled off to the side near the shore of the bank where it was gentler and slower. As we continued our conversation, we realized that each of us was in the same water and experienced it very differently. This helped us have compassion for each other as well as for ourselves. We acknowledged the differences in flow, cadence, and depth, and how the responses would be different depending on our location. Turbulent scenarios had different size barriers or obstructions in front of them. We can't change where people are in their lives, but we can have compassion, understanding, and the ability to see things differently instead of just looking or comparing our location to others.

In a river, or any body of water, there are obstructions that create an eddy. An eddy is a circular current that swirls directly behind a rock or obstruction. This has less momentum and force in it. The water is swirling in the opposite direction of the water flow which creates, if you will, a resting place. A pause. A moment. The eddy will take you out of the current momentum and slow you down. Then after a while it will transition you into a second eddy that feeds you back into the flow of the river.

I believe this is what healing is like. There are times when you are engaged, practicing self-care, moving forward, and suddenly you hit a wall, or an obstruction of sorts appears. Typically, this is our next piece of healing waiting to be healed, but the pain hits first, so we need the eddy to slow things down so we can face what we need to face.

As a business owner, I used to get worried when my business started ebbing but after a while, I started paying attention to my own energy, capacity, and emotional equilibrium. I started to challenge myself to embrace the ebb. What I found during these times is that I moved out of logistic practices, and gave myself time and space to review, rest, reevaluate, rejuvenate, and respond to things differently. This typically brought out the creative side of me, and helped restore my energy and capacity to ramp business up as promptings, and inspired actions showed up more and more. The next thing I know, I am back in the flow in this beautiful space of creation and stretching toward new growth in my business. In many, many ways, the ebb is still unnerving and very uncomfortable but like I've mentioned, change and growth live where we feel uncomfortable.

I took my business perspective and applied it, more and more into my life, and realized I needed to do the same thing; embrace the ebb. Whenever a barrier comes up it means there is something to be healed. Healing isn't easy because we often run into resistance, or the obstruction. We resist what's unknown, what's unfamiliar. That's why we need the ebb. We need time to identify what's in front of us. We need to embrace the pause so we can listen in more than one way. Our body talks to us and shows us where we are stressed or resisting. Our communication can flag how we are acting out our pain and not speaking our truth. Our sleep, diet, attitude, actions, or inactions are indicators to what's real and at the origin of our healing.

I watched Tony Robbins's film; *I am not your Guru* on Netflix and noted when he said that life changes in moments. He confirmed for me that life changes in moments; however, it may take us years to get to that moment because we have not reached the point where we want to change what we're experiencing. I found this to be so true for me and for my family.

We tolerate a lot of pain. In fact, I was discussing this with my husband last night about how we have a very high tolerance for pain hence why we suffered for so long. Even my husband has tolerated some physical pain and discomfort up to a point that the medical solution has been drastic. His body created the "moment." If we had responded earlier, he would not have gone through such intense treatment and recovery.

Writing this book is a moment that took me over 10 years to reach. I first tried in 2014 but was overwhelmed by the pain of my memories, and navigating life when fragments of trauma still surfaced. By 2022, I wrote the first draft, and I encountered yet another moment that required deeper healing. Though writing was profoundly cathartic, it also stirred up parts of me that needed mending, including wounds from before my daughter's trauma.

Consider your own healing journey like a river. There are sections where the flow is smooth and forward moving, while others may get caught behind obstacles, becoming turbulent or chaotic. Some parts may gently guide you into a pause or an easier rhythm. Life's river is filled with ebbs, flows, blockages, and breakthroughs—each moment is part of your journey and your personal healing.

So, here's my invitation to you: Take a moment to reflect on these questions. Are tolerating pain or suffering? Do you feel trapped, as if life will never change? Even if it feels true now, remember—it doesn't have to be permanent. Healing comes with its own ebb and flow. The question is, how long will you tolerate your own pain before you embrace change?

Imagine how much better your life could be if you choose to listen to those moments when you feel prompted. Change begins with you. It might be scary, uncomfortable, and filled with unknowns, but it can also be the key to transforming your life—the "a-ha" moment you've been waiting for. Write it out, purge your emotions, or map out everything that's causing your suffering in the moment. Let it come up! Healing isn't ONE destination—it is a journey of destinations marked by vulnerability, courage, and healing.

It's okay to feel what you feel; it's not wrong. You may even get emotional, angry, apathetic, or even feel confused or frustrated by what you feel. Don't judge—just notice what you feel. What matters most is what you do with those emotions.

If you're completely angry and need to get it out. Find an "Angry room" where you can safely destroy things. Write an angry letter and tear it up. Punch or scream into a pillow. Find healthy ways to express your anger and hurt so that you release what no longer serves you.

Do you need to cry? Read a book, watch a movie, talk to a friend, or do what you need to help you release your tears. I believe tears and screams are words that cannot be expressed. There are some parking lots that have received a lot of my tears. When I need to cry, I find a private place for me to just release them. Cry until I'm done. And then I sit in the quiet as if to wrap myself in a hug of relief.

And as for apathy, understanding apathy was a turning point in my healing journey. I remember feeling overwhelmed by a deep sense of apathy—nothing mattered to me. My daily mantra became, "I don't care," and even though it troubled me, I couldn't shake the feeling. I confided in a friend about how unlike myself I felt, and she responded, "But it is you. There's a reason you're feeling this way—you just need to uncover the source."

As I shared my experience with friends and a community of women I belong to, I began to see that apathy was serving a purpose. It was helping me detach from everything around me, allowing me the space to CHOOSE what truly mattered. This period of apathy taught me valuable lessons about self-love, and the importance of distinguishing between what is mine to handle, and what is not.

If you're feeling apathetic or disconnected, know that this feeling can be a guide. It's not a dead end, but rather an opportunity to reassess and realign with what genuinely matters to you. Embrace it as part of your journey toward healing and self-discovery.

Next, I want you to make a commitment to NOT be tolerant of suffering. When I finally saw hope break into my life, I had learned to make three commitments to myself.

1. Show up every day and not run away; instead face the day.

2. Reach out and create customized support.

3. And finally, stop beating myself up.

I want you to learn to identify how you want to show up every day. I also want you to envision your life without pain. What if you stopped tolerating the things you are tolerating? What if you could live without this pain? What would have to change? What would your life look like? Be like? What would you be experiencing? What do you really want? Often, we don't know how to say what we want, so reverse engineer it. Make a list of things that you don't want and then translate them into the wants that resonate with you.

Here are some of my own translations:

I DON'T WANT	VS.	I DO WANT
I don't want to die.	VS.	I want to learn how to regulate emotional and mental pain.
I don't want to feel lonely.	VS.	I want to connect with people.
I don't want to keep worrying.	VS.	I want to learn what is mine to change.

I don't want to live like this.	**vs.**	I want to learn how to put healthy boundaries in place.
I don't like feeling this sluggish and tired.	**vs.**	I want to have vibrant health.
I don't always want to feel scared.	**vs.**	I want to learn how to feel and be empowered.

When getting clear on your wants, make sure you choose the statement that best resonates with you. The ebb and flow of healing is about listening to YOU, your body, and your soul. This requires you to be quiet during the ebb so you can listen internally for what you need and want. Giving yourself permission to take time for yourself is crucial so that you can pause and be present with your thought evolutions. There are iterations of healing. We heal only as deep as we allow ourselves to go, so there might be repetition in the process. However, if you're ready to go deep, and get to the root of it then I say go for it. Shorten your length of suffering!

My life changed in a moment while I was driving for the truth about suffering being a choice. When I had my epiphany, my life changed in the very next breath. The part that took the longest was getting to that moment. I had tolerated suffering and didn't realize it. I thought this was how my life was always going to be. I had a choice. I could look at things differently, as well as respond differently, and that is what I did. I said, "Enough!" to suffering and pain, and became hungry for increasing hope and happiness in my life.

In my healing journey, I have gone to therapy when I need it. I've taken classes that I'm interested in to strengthen my own talents and gifts. I read all kinds of books for personal and professional development. I have been a part of or joined like-minded communities to help me expand and grow. I learn from my clients as they shift and grow from our work together. I attend personal and group retreats to spend time in quiet. I meditate, go for walks, and carve out weekends for quiet and visioning. I pray, give daily gratitude, and practice the power of visualization.

I still have times that I lose my bearings. However, they are shorter lived because I have learned what steps I need to take to ground myself, get my bearings, and get back on my feet. I move at the pace of a turtle, so please know healing can come to you too. My hope is that your tolerance for pain and suffering will be shortened by the decisions you make. You can do this.

My life's lesson has been learning how to be vulnerable. Not an easy or fun lesson. I have had to take baby steps to feel safe. Practicing vulnerability one step at a time is what helped me get to the point that I could write this book. Practicing and being vulnerable in small bits and pieces helped me gain support I never knew existed.

Listen, you're going to trip, stumble, and fall in life; that is a given. The difference is whether you get up or not. This is your most powerful strategy. Embrace your brokenness knowing that you will be stronger because of it. Don't look at life as all or nothing, instead look at life as a powerful rhythm of ebb and flow, like the river and all its landscape. Learn to go internally, to listen, and to know your truth.

You have everything within you to heal, to empower yourself, and to mend areas of breakage in your mind, heart, body, and soul. Surround yourself with customized support so you aren't doing it alone. Know that there are people out there who hold the highest and best for you. They love you unconditionally and hold space for you to learn how to give yourself permission so you can fully be who you came here to be at the soul level.

"Trust the wisdom within you. Your inner guidance is your compass, always pointing you toward love, truth, and spiritual growth."

—WAYNE DYER

THE INTERNAL
COMPASS

I believe everyone has an internal compass; the difference is whether the compass is guided by an internal perpetrator or the master goddess within. The words internal perpetrator may seem harsh but be patient. Let me explain. We can be excessively hard on ourselves, for some, almost relentless punishing of the worst kind. We worry too much about what others think, try to please everyone but ourselves, and fear failure or blame to the point of losing sight of who we are. This is exactly what happened to me—I felt like I was losing myself and the very ground I once stood on.

Barbara Huson, author of *Sacred Success*, said it well during one of her group sessions. She said, "Success is an inside job." I couldn't agree more. When we align ourselves with our true north, everything becomes easier. There is less overwhelm, less to remember, and a more powerful purpose, connection, activity, and growth.

Growing up, I wasn't connected to my internal compass. I followed instructions without question, adhered to expectations, and complied with the rules to keep myself safe. I was guided by an internal perpetrator who fed me lies and tried to dismantle my self-worth. When my daughter's trauma occurred, it didn't take much to disrupt my compass once again and leave me feeling lost.

Think about a compass with the needle pointing to true north as your power center. True north represents where you stand in life when grounded and empowered. During the trauma, if I asked myself where I was in relation to my true north, I would have said the needle was pointing in the opposite direction from where I needed to be. I was so far out of alignment that it's no wonder I got lost in my mental storm. Without a connection to my compass, I was directing myself away from my center rather than toward it.

When my clients feel lost, I use the compass analogy to help them. I ask them to envision their internal compass and identify where the needle is pointing in relation to their true north. I then ask, "What steps can you take to realign with your true north? What is one action you can take to feel more centered?" Connecting with our internal compass can help guide us back to our true north and help us find our way again.

Importance of Faith

A big part of my healing journey was to redefine and establish what faith means to me. I believe I have a soul that it is divinely guided by an energy that is bigger than me. I believe there is an afterlife, and we have the ability to learn how to connect with those who have crossed over. I have learned to listen and to expand my intuitiveness, to listen to my gut and inner knowingness, and continue to learn how to quiet my mind and listen. I have experienced the quiet voice inside of me that knows my truth. My ego talks loudly, especially when I'm scared because it is trying to protect me. I am grateful for this because it helps me discern what is true. Whether you call this higher power God, Spirit, the Universe, or Energy, know that you get to choose to believe or not believe. It is not for me to tell you.

As for myself, I believe God is bigger than what is taught hence why I like to use Spirit or the Universe. I am surrounded by guidance. I have to believe in something bigger than myself because people who are able to survive the most horrific situations in life are miracles in action. You are more than a survivor or secondary survivor. You are love at the deepest soul level, and you have so much to give from what you have experienced. I wouldn't be the person I am today if I hadn't had painful teachers like my mom, my daughter, and her perpetrator. I wouldn't have the tools that I am sharing with you and with my clients if I hadn't lived through my darkness. I believe our most powerful tools come from the darkest places. They unearth us, and at the same time, we unearth the miracles.

This healing journey taught me to send my mom, who crossed over in 2012, love and gratitude. I had hated her a lot in my life and blamed her for a lot of my pain. She was a serious threat to my mental health. She made my life miserable, but I cannot deny her credit for being responsible for the person I am today. Living with my mom made me determined to respond to things differently. I learned through my spiritual studies that there is purpose in everything. We came here to learn and to help others. My learning was painful, but I am able to help others move out of pain more quickly and equip them to become unstoppable because of those lessons. How can I deny the power of the learning? The outcome is lived by me and others who have experienced the work of connecting to their internal compass. I have seen clients shift and release things they have carried for years.

I had to commit to doing the internal work so I could show up in this world to serve the people I am here to help. I had to learn to listen to myself so I could wake up to all that was possible and step forward in my life.

I learned how to have GRIT, which I translated into an acronym:

- **G:** Grounded in who I came here to be and to serve,
- **R:** Resilient in my mindset,
- **I:** Innovative in my approach, and
- **T:** Tenaciously committed to my dreams.

You have an internal compass and my question for you is, who is guiding your compass? Is it an internal perpetrator holding lies against you or is it your master goddess within who holds your truth of who you came here to be? What can you do to help you align with your true north?

I know there are times that you might want to quit, don't. Know that you can shift your perspective to look at life differently. Know that there are people waiting for you and what you bring to this world.

When I am experiencing a trigger or struggling, I read my Letter of Courage. I wrote this back when I was just starting my coaching business. I was afraid I would give up on myself, so I sat down, listened, and wrote this letter from my soul to help me get back to center and keep going.

What if you write your own Letter of Courage? What if this helps you get grounded and centered? What if this removes the barrier that keeps you playing small? What if you play to win in life rather than playing to not lose? What if your own pain is calling you to your own greatness?

I've included my instructions for how to write your own Letter of Courage. Until you have written your own, I am lending this letter to you when you need it.

Dear Friend,

I know you are tired, frustrated, and ready to quit. This journey has had some very painful parts for you, and I know that's the reason why you are saying, "I can't do this anymore. I'm not worth it." That's why I'm writing this letter to you before you quit.

I want you to see what I see. I see a person who is powerful beyond measure. A person who doesn't hesitate to step in and give a hand-up to someone in need. You cheer the actions of others to reach their highest potential and biggest dreams.

You have a unique way, my friend, of connecting people to what makes them feel priceless and like any dream is possible. You're a leader, a motivator, and a game changer. Nothing has ever taken you down and, believe me, I know how life has tried. I know you have fallen over, and over, and over again. Do not tally these falls as points of failure, instead count them as your marks for success. For each time you fell down, you stood up...and stood up... and stood up. Your courage is limitless. Most people would have become scared and stayed on the ground—not you, not now. You ARE standing strong.

You, my friend, are standing on sacred ground. A ground that possesses every dream, every desire, every treasure that you have thought about, felt in your heart, and have not yet comprehended. The key is to have the courage to take the next step. No one is here to take it for you or from you, nor are they capable of doing so. You are the only one who holds the key. Your inner gifts and the world are waiting...waiting for YOU.

So please, before you quit, ask yourself if you want to leave these gifts untouched before the end of this career, business or before the end of your life. I guarantee that the world has already opened up to you and is standing to cheer your arrival. I am with you always, my friend, and will love you forever.

From the deepest part of my heart, I love you.

Your Soul

Letter of Courage

In life, we need that stopgap that keeps us on track so that we don't go completely off the rails due to our mindset. Many times, in life, our ego gets in the way, and we start playing to NOT lose instead of playing to WIN! This Letter of Courage puts the emotional charges in check and reminds you of who you are and who you came here to be. This is your letter to remind yourself that you are here to play to win!

We all have moments or days that we want to quit. Don't. I am asking you to write a Letter of Courage, to help you understand the decision you are about to make and the outcomes that will result from it. Also, know the difference between giving up on your dreams and giving up a habit or thought that keeps you safe. Life isn't about playing small—it's about answering the call to greatness.

This letter is so important that it should be placed in a cabinet like a fire extinguisher labeled, "Break Glass in Case of Emergency" because on the day you are contemplating saying, "I quit!"—you may very well be quitting on your dreams. NOW THAT'S AN EMERGENCY!

Let's get started!

Circle Map

Get a blank piece of paper, think about a day in your life that went really, really bad and brought up all these emotions— strong enough to have you say, "I quit. I can't do this anymore. I'm done...." What is the sentence that keeps repeating inside your head that is beating you up? Write THAT sentence in the center of your paper and circle it. Now, think about the situation again that brought up that sentence. How did you feel? Write down all of the thoughts and emotions as you come up with them. Circle EACH thought and EACH emotion. Keep going until you are complete.

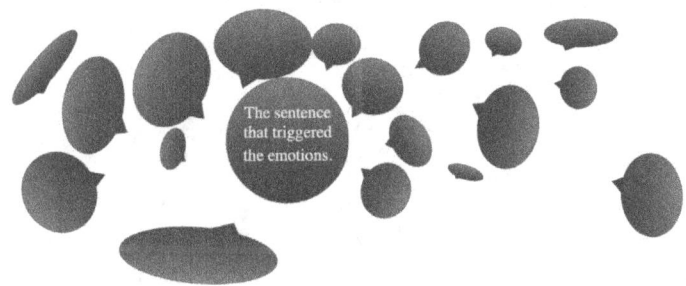

It is these emotional charges that lead us to making decisions that we may regret or react in a way that is not working from our best mindset. You're human. It is important to recognize these emotions. The key is to take the charge out of them so you can move to a clearer place of thinking and evaluate what's going on. See what needs to change...typically it is mindset and approach.

Letter Format:

Consider writing your letter by hand or, at the minimum, having the letter physically arrive to you through snail mail (physical mailbox).

Part 1:

The first part of the letter is going to address your struggles and the emotions that are attached to them. You need to connect with the emotions so you can take the charge out of them. When you're in that bad day of your life, what do you feel like you are doing? Are you standing in quicksand? Did you get knocked off your feet? Were you blindsided and now you can't breathe? Is someone trying to take you down? What's going on in this pain? What are you feeling? Look at your CIRCLE MAP. Get specific on your struggle so that when you read it you can say, "Yep, that's me. That's my bad day all the way around."

What do you want to do? Do you want to scream? Cuss? Tear something apart? Do you want to go into your cave and never come out? Cry? Punch something? What? Describe what you go through and all the attempts you have made to keep going. This is all leading up to the point where you want to quit. It's like turning in a letter of resignation.

Part 2:

The Turning Point: Now say, "Before you turn in your letter of resignation, I want you to see what I see.... I see you as a person who...." Capitalize on your strengths, courage, and determination. Give examples of you getting back up on your feet, your resiliency! This is where your tough love best friend is standing next to you while you're face down on the ground. They're yelling, cheering, "GET UP! You can do this! I said get up!" Use the words that motivate you to stand up, keep going, to understand how much courage it takes to stand back up again and take the next step. If you need to do a CIRCLE MAP for this process, do it. Give yourself that motivating sentence that fills your heart with passion and gets you going. What are the thoughts and feelings attached to this sentence?

Part 3:

Remind yourself that you are the ONLY ONE who possesses the gifts that only you can bring to this life, your work, and to the world. You may know people who offer something similar, or even exactly what you offer in their life's work. The differentiator is YOU! Your strengths can make a measurable difference that makes you stand out or deliver the unexpected. Your approach can be as different as your fingerprints, most everyone has them, but they are different enough to identify only you as the owner. What is the imprint you will make in this life for yourself and others? It doesn't have to be big; it just has to be YOU.

Part 4:

End the letter stating that you are fully supported and embracing what you love. Then sign it in a way that resonates with you.

Part 5:

Mail the letter to yourself. Let me say that again, mail the letter to yourself. And I do mean snail mail. Not through email. There is something powerful about receiving your letter in the physical sense and opening it up to receive it.

Part 6:

This letter is your safeguard—to prevent you from abandoning your dreams. It serves as a compelling reminder to keep going and to recommit to your dreams and aspirations.

I have my Letter of Courage close by. Even when I was writing my own coaching program AND as I wrote this book, I carried the letter with me readily available to read. Now I'm going to tell you to do the same thing. Place your letter in a location where you can easily access it in case of an emergency. [Break glass!]

I still have my Letter of Courage. I've carried it with me when I'm feeling uncomfortable with the changes I need to make. I read it after a disappointing end to a business venture. I've read it when I wanted to quit writing this book. My letter is my stopgap. When I read it, I can feel myself click back in and get back on track with what's mine to do. This may be one of the most important letters you ever receive in the mail.

Write it. Mail it. Receive it. Keep it handy.

"Simply with a change of mind you can change your life."

—DEEPAK CHOPRA

"The paradox of trauma is that it has both the power to destroy and the power to transform and resurrect."

—PETER A. LEVINE

AFFIRMATIONS +
MANIFESTO

Our minds are powerful, and I knew I needed affirmations that would help raise my energy and vibration for visualizing what I want. I used Keynote, similar to PowerPoint, to insert my affirmations on individual slides. Then I gathered photos that imbued the feelings I wanted to match with each affirmation. Once I put it all together, I exported the slides as a video with music attached. I use this video to say and feel my affirmations. I am a very visual person so having my affirmations play in a beautiful visual way helps strengthen my feelings. And when we can see and feel something, it helps to strengthen our beliefs. These affirmations and the video are like my Letter of Courage. They help me to keep going.

Affirmations:

Read these affirmations, say them out loud to yourself, look in the mirror and say them. Write one on your mirror with a dry erase marker to help feed your brain every day. Record yourself saying them so you can listen with your eyes closed, and absorb the wisdom into your heart. Do what helps you. I encourage you to create your own affirmations.

I also decided to write a manifesto envisioning an online community coming together to have empowered connections and conversations about secondary trauma. What if having these connections and conversations helps reduce the length of pain an individual experiences? What if it creates healing in ways we have not yet comprehended? What if it has a ripple effect that creates positive impact? What if you wrote a personal manifesto to strengthen who you came here to be? No matter what, I want you to have fun surrounding yourself with words that empower your thoughts. Remember words wield power!

I AM LISTENING

When my ego speaks first and loudest, I am reminded to stop, be still, and listen to my soul.

I AM COMMITTED

I am tenaciously committed to my dreams and my desires!

I AM SAFE

My healthy expression of anger galvanizes who I am and allows me to release what does not serve me.

I AM CONNECTED

I am connecting to my soul's wisdom. I am living from a deeper place at a higher vibration.

I AM RESPONDING BEAUTIFULLY

When I face challenges, I can respond by asking to see things differently.

I AM A CHANGE AGENT

I know it's okay to be scared and uncomfortable; that's where change and growth stretches me.

I AM COURAGEOUS

I am courageously stepping into the life I desire and asking for what I want.

I AM ALIGNED

I am living in alignment with my soul. I live in the powerful interplay of ebb and flow.

I DREAM BIG

I know who I am and what I want. I am expressing myself unapologetically in who I came here to BE.

I LIVE IN ABUNDANCE

I am making a significant amount of money having the time of my life!

I AM STANDING STRONG

I own my sacred space to stand and move the world!

I AM TRANSFORMING

I am surrendering to my dreams so I can learn how to fly!

I BELIEVE IN ME

I am connecting to my soul's wisdom and know my truth.

I AM UNSTOPPABLE

I know what it takes for me to get back up on my feet and to keep going.

I AM ENOUGH!

(To see the clip with music visit: https://www.janetredford.com/awakening-soulpreneurs)

Affirmations + Manifesto

"If you embrace possibility thinking, your dreams will go from molehill to mountain size, and because you believe in possibilities, you put yourself in position to achieve them."

—JOHN C. MAXWELL

MANIFESTO: SURRENDERING TO YOUR DREAMS —YOUR SACRED BLUEPRINT

In the majestic presence of life's mountain, our DREAMS are the peaks beckoning us to ascend. This manifesto is a Call to Surrender— to climb with courage, facing the challenges and embracing the wins, until we stand fully embodied at the summit of our SOUL'S aspirations.

Embrace your VISION with uncompromising passion, for it guides you through the mist of uncertainty, like distant peaks illuminating the path to your highest potential. Release fear and doubt, the treacherous slopes that threaten to derail your ascent, and step forward with unwavering FAITH in your ability to conquer.

SURRENDER to the rhythm of the climb, trusting each foothold to lead you closer to your dreams. Every stumble becomes a lesson, every setback a chance to grow stronger. Take inspired action with each step, fueled by the vision of standing tall upon the summit.

Cultivate resilience, drawing STRENGTH from the earth beneath your feet, the sky above your head, and the unfailing faith in your heart.

The journey to the summit is not without its trials, but with resilience, you rise to meet every challenge.

When at last you reach this summit, let your heart stay open and EXPAND with joy. Celebrate the victory of surrendering to your dreams, knowing that you have reached the pinnacle of what's possible.

By Surrendering to your SOUL, you will find yourself living from a deeper place at a higher vibration with endless possibilities stretching out before you. This is your SACRED blueprint.

THANK YOU!

You have been on a journey of healing. I am grateful to share parts of mine in hopes that it has brought some understanding, useful tools and relief to your pain. Know that there are powerful gifts hidden in the darkness waiting to be unearthed by you. Know that life can be more healing, more powerful, and more deeply experienced because you are more than a secondary survivor. Your life is meant to be lived more beautifully. Go live it. Be it. Own it.

"*We have to continue to learn. We have to be open. And we have to be ready to release our knowledge in order to come to a higher understanding of reality.*"

—THICK NHAT HANH

NAMASTE

My soul honors your soul. I honor the place in you where the entire universe resides. I honor the light, love, truth, beauty, and peace within you, because it is also within me. In sharing these things, we are united, we are the same, we are ONE.

"Gratitude is when memory is stored in the heart and not in the mind."

—LIONEL HAMPTON

ACKNOWLEDGMENTS

To my husband, Duane Redford. There will never be enough words to express the deep gratitude I have for you. You are my rock. Thank you for always having my back. I love you from the deepest part of my soul. —B.B.L.K.P.

To my daughter Allie. Thank you for choosing life—for never giving up. You are my sacred teacher whose life has taught me what's possible when we allow our hearts to evolve and expand.

To my son, Parker. Thank you for your unending love and support. You challenge me, the turtle, to come out of my shell and risk vulnerability. You demand that I be me. Thank you for your intensity.

To Allie, Parker, and my grandchildren. I love you more than all the stars in the sky and beyond! My heart is always with you.

At times, being on this journey can feel very lonely, and yet as I look back and realize just how many people over the years have helped me walk the path toward healing, I am humbled. You showed light when I only saw darkness. You guided me when I needed clarity. You challenged me to see what was bigger than me. You poured love and support into me and my family's life from the smallest act of kindness to the most generous act of love that is mind-boggling. I cannot begin to list all the people that have been there for us throughout the years, as I am afraid of missing someone in this moment. Please know that I know who you are, and I hold the deepest level of gratitude in my heart and soul for you. I would not be where I am today without you.

AUTHOR BIO

Janet Redford is a speaker, coach and mentor dedicated to helping others achieve personal freedom by breaking through limiting beliefs and aligning mindset with action. As a former Sign Language Interpreter, Janet elevated her profession and mentored interns, fostering growth, and excellence. Her journey through a traumatic family experience, involving sexual abuse of her child, reshaped her understanding of healing and personal development. This challenging time inspired her to create transformative work for her clients, emphasizing that while the process isn't easy, it is deeply powerful. Janet believes that true growth requires confronting inner barriers and making courageous shifts.

Janet is the founder of MBodi3™, a coaching practice designed to help clients master their passion and purpose by fully embodying all they are meant to be. Her approach combines mindset work with strategic action, empowering her clients to break through their limitations and achieve lasting change. Though the work can be intense, it is this very intensity that leads to profound transformation. Janet lives in Colorado, where she enjoys spending time with her husband, children, grandchildren, and dog Rip.

REFERENCES

American SPCC. n.d. *Preventing Child Sexual Abuse as Parents & Caregivers*. Accessed 2024. https://americanspcc.org/sexual-child-abuse/.

Giordano, Amanda L. 2021. *Why Trauma Can Lead to Addiction*. Edited by Vanessa Lancaster. 09 25. Accessed 2024. : https://www.psychologytoday.com/us/blog/understanding-addiction/202109/why-trauma-can-lead-to-addiction.

National Center for Victims of Crime. n.d. *Grooming Dynamic*. Accessed 2024. https://victimsofcrime.org/grooming-dynamic/.

RAINN. n.d. *Child Sexual Abuse*. Accessed 2024. https://rainn.org/articles/child-sexual-abuse.